Lady Moratorium

&

The Purposeful Practice of Fine

By: Dani Hartung

Lady Moratorium & The Purposeful Practice of Fine

Table of Contents

Foreword

By Julia Chestnut

I met Dani Hartung on a blind date.

The year was 2015 and I was a junior in college at Kansas State University, where I was struggling to balance academics, personal life, and the unique challenges of being a Division I NCAA athlete on the women's rowing team. One afternoon, I sat across from my fellow rower and friend, Anna, in a Starbucks. I was probably venting about some relationship issue with all the dramatics and gusto I am well-known for, when Anna (who is deliberately known for her lack of dramatics) said abruptly "You know, you should really talk to my friend Dani about this. You're pretty similar; I think the two of you would hit it off."

So, I put on my big-girl panties and nervously sent Dani a friend request on Facebook. "This is so weird," I thought to myself. "She's probably going to think I'm a freak." When Dani accepted my request, I messaged her, explained who I was and sheepishly asked if she would want to hang out sometime. To my surprise, she enthusiastically agreed. We set up a day to grab brunch at a local cafe, and the rest was history. After some initial nerves and a few cups of coffee, we were chatting away like we had known each other from birth.

I imagine this is how reading this book will feel for many of you, like a conversation with an old friend. I have never felt more comfortable than in the presence of Dani Hartung, and in her writing, her warm tone and unprecedented openness create a precious sense of familiarity for her audience. We often feel safest to be our truest selves and express our deepest emotions when we spend time with another person who is willing to do the same, to lay all cards on the table and say "Here I am, in all my failings and my glory. This is me." In these situations of mutual vulnerability, someone has to be the one to go first - and Hartung has taken the leap with grace and honesty in this book.

Just like our friendship in real life, no topic is taboo for Hartung as an author. She courageously delves into all the things people yearn to speak candidly about: money, mental health, romance, career ambitions... Even poop. (Just wait for Chapter 14. It's a good one.) For as long as I have had the privilege of knowing her, Hartung's ability to reflect and self-assess with great candor and wit continues to be a breath of fresh air. Her writing is the voice of love and validation for those who cannot yet give it to themselves, and I suspect this book will be a refuge of compassion for the world's exhausted and lost -- which, if we're honest, is all of us at some point in our lives.

To every athlete, every child prodigy, every single parent, lonely widow, burnt-out businessman, questioning philosopher, insecure teen, over-achiever, under-achiever, and everything else in between: this book is for YOU. To everyone who has ever needed a pep talk, a pat on the back, or a swift kick in the pants: you'll get all three in this book. And lastly, to anyone who has ever looked around at the life they have created for themselves and wondered "Well... Is this it?", I encourage you to embark on the journey to "finding your Fine" with Dani Hartung as your guide. You won't be sorry you did.

moratorium

noun **plural -ria** (-пǝ) *or* **-riums**
1. a legally authorized postponement of the fulfilment of an obligation
2. an agreed suspension of activity

Who the Hell Are You?

I'm sitting in a coffee shop, scrolling through Instagram and hoping for some spontaneous inspiration to strike me, like a lightning bolt from the heavens. I am hella drowsy from the migraine meds I took this morning, and I'm also anxiously grumpy that the rough draft of my book isn't finished yet. My vanilla flavored coffee is delicious, and I revel in this fact for a stolen moment...until the family two tables over yammers on about nothing specific or discernable, in the echoing acoustics of the high-ceilinged building. I honestly love kids, but I'm about to go entirely Hulk Hogan on these parents for not teaching them the art of shutting the hell up during breakfast.

Clearly, I am grouchy today.

But today, I am still here.

I work to give myself credit for driving to this coffee shop from my house, for taking the time out of my precious few days of holiday break to work on a project so close to my heart, when I easily could have slept through the entire week. And I strain to remind myself of my daily affirmations:

1. I am smart and capable.
2. I am beautiful.
3. I am funny and worth people's time.
4. I am fit and strong.
5. I am brave enough to love without expectations.
6. I am bigger and better than anything that has ever hurt me.
7. I am worth more than my mistakes.
8. *I love myself.*

I take a deep breath, and another swig of scrumptious coffee. I manage to offer a weak and slightly forced smile to the bubbly, bustling family as they rise to leave the shop. I wake up my laptop screen once more with a wispy swipe of my finger across the touchpad.

And I write.

....

At the ripe, old age of 25, I find myself in an almost constant state of searching. That said, I don't know that I can pinpoint exactly *what* I'm searching for -- except, that is, what a more self-assured person might refer to as "the point of it all." If you're a reader over the age of 35, I know what you're (already) thinking: *And here we have it, yet again: the pessimistic musings of another snivelling snowflake millennial with a four-year university degree and no desire to join the bureaucracy. This oughta be good.*

We-he-he-hellll, okay, Boomer! Do you know what I say to you, my government-subsidized-college-tuition-and-likely-the-sneaky-type-of-prejudiced friend?

Whoa. Um...*ahem.* Sorry. Actually, let me just back up for a quick second.

I think it's important to admit up front, right at the outset of this book, that I am hyper-aware of my own insecurity. And emotional sensitivity. And high-achievement complex. *Sheesh*, let's get back on track, shall we? Basically, I'm incredibly likely to lash out at the first inclination of people's judgement and/or project my own preconceived notions onto others, wallowing in my own assumption that they are doing the same to me.

What I mean to say is that, even though one of the things I'm searching for is the answer to the question, "How does one display this 'confidence' trait I've heard tell of?"...I'm also fully cognizant of the fact that my *lack* of confidence has stemmed largely from a self-fulfilling prophecy therein. I often tend to come across to others quickly as defensive and guarded. I suppose this is a learned self-protective behavior that I should really chat about with Gina, my counselor. I have been talking with her regularly, though, which is a measure that has noticeably (and *blessedly*) improved the quality of my life and self-concept.

So far, we have uncovered my knee-jerk, anxiety-fueled desire to take up as little space as possible in the lives of others (which is super difficult as a five-ten, 190-pound lady!). More to the point, though, I have a hard time feeling worthy of my own space, which I can't *help* but occupy. The cognitive dissonance that these feelings have created has inconveniently manifested itself as (for example) my need to proofread professional emails six to ten times before sending them, or my habitual use of the words "just" and "sorry." Or, the worst of all -- my pitiful, self-deprecating assumption that, after any social encounter (regardless of the apparent quality of the overall interaction) that the other party involved in this exchange likely could not *wait* until it was finally over so that they could leave this weirdly clingy, annoying, slightly-too-loud girl behind them.

This is one of many issues that I'm working through with Gina. However, something she said recently got me thinking:

"People send typos in emails all the time. It's not the end of the world, and no one is going to think less of you if you make a mistake. You don't need to expend so much energy worrying about your emails [or other trivial things]. You need to remember that, no matter what you send, it's going to be fine."

Hold the phone. What was that word?

FINE...?

For me (and, I assume, at least a few other people), the concept of Fine has a negative connotation. Fine means that, yes, you technically did the job you set out to do...but you didn't blow anyone's mind. You didn't break any records. You didn't *win*. I am no stranger to the pursuit of victory. In fact, somewhere, over the course of my life, achievement became the most important aspect of everything I did. Like, if there was an award for *Most Likely to Work Herself to an Untimely Death in the Pursuit of Perfection and, Hence, the Approval of Others*, I would nab that shit in a second. Oh, yeah.

But when Gina used the word "fine," I shook my head and rattled my brain around a little bit, cartoon-character-style, to help me comprehend exactly what she meant. Because when Gina used the word "fine," I could have sworn it almost sounded like she meant "*good*." Good? Fine? As in, "not the

G.O.A.T., but yet still not at all bad, and, in fact, quite acceptable? Maybe even, like...*healthier*"? What the hell.

This revelation -- this teensy, semantics-based distinction -- turned my world on its head. For *years*, I had assumed that I should not pursue any task, dream, or conversation unless I had at least some assurance that I would either be or produce the best possible version of whatever was expected of me. If this was not possible, or at least likely, I was struck with the paralyzing fear of failure and my blood would run cold with the twisted belief that I was now worthless. (Also, I possess a decided flair for the dramatic, but I'm trying to be more confident about it, so...back off!) This obsessive drive kept me constantly striving for the top place on the podium, regardless of the arena. In the words of the great Ricky Bobby, "If ya ain't first, you're last!"

That's how I felt. If I wasn't the best (the favorite, the record-holder, the prodigy), then who the hell was *I* to take up space? Who was I to laugh too loud, to speak confidently in departmental meetings, or to presume worthiness of love? Of friendship? Of respect? But...what if I tried Fine on for size? What if *that* was the standard, not born out of near-failure but in *aspirational* terms? What would I be worth *then*?

It was this question (and the urgent, loving words of beloved author Rachel Hollis) which inspired me to write this book. I have quite literally *always* wanted to be an author -- I'm talking, ever since my first fifth-grade creative writing assignment, and maybe even before. I have started stories, written outlines, created characters, and crumpled half-scribbled papers a million-bajillion times. But my stories never seemed quite important enough, or original enough, or captivating enough. And I couldn't possibly dare to ask an audience of readers to give two shits about the one story that I was qualified to share and wanted most desperately to tell: mine.

Why would anyone care about that? My story isn't even *done*, for crying out loud! I am imperfect. I certainly haven't "come out on the other side" of my anxiety or my insecurity (clearly). But, perhaps, the unfinished nature of my story is the most relatable point.

In her TED Talk entitled, "We Find Each Other in the Details," one of my favorite poets, Olivia Gatwood, taught me that poetry and its subsequent performance is "one of the deepest forms of gluttony." To ask someone else to listen to a story about your life -- one that doesn't look, on the surface, like anything they have experienced themselves -- sounds so selfish. It sounds like an act that would take up a *whole* lot of space.

But it is in this space, Olivia reasoned, we are able to make the deepest connections with our audience -- with *each other*. Sure, your story, with all its flaws, frustrations, and scary parts, may not be exactly like anything your audience has seen or experienced firsthand. But how have they *felt*? Have they ever felt imperfect or angry or afraid, in the same ways that you have? These commonalities are the basis of human connection, but the key to unlocking the potential for such connection is the *willingness* to spread out, speak up, and assert the value of your very own story, regardless of its worth to humanity as a whole.

So, this is me. Taking a deep breath, fumbling with the microphone, and sweating a little bit (a lotta bit) on my upper lip.

I am preparing to read you a poem.

This poem doesn't rhyme, it doesn't offer much in the way of absolutes, and it feels like one of the biggest emotional risks I've ever taken. It includes, in each chapter, a suggested book that has captured my heart and attention, as well as sporadic commentary and reassurances from friends whose real-life presence and advice have made all the difference in my journey. This poem is the culmination of the delicious marriage between my own emotional energy and the intertwined spiritual vibrations of the strong, beautiful beings I call my friends.

I hope that you relish this poem, as I do. But I also know that the reality is, you might hate it.

And you know what I'm learning? That would be...*fine*. I will be fine. And my story is, at the very least, worth the chance that I might make someone else feel connected and un-alone.

So, Fine is exactly where my story begins.

Chapter #1:

What I Mean by "Fine"

I am lying in my California King-sized, memory foam bed, which sounds like the world's most pretentious way of saying that something is simply "comfortable." But, regardless of this gluttonous luxury, I am unmistakably wide awake. In fact, my brain is moving a mile a minute, as if I washed down some ADHD meds with Red Bull after a six-course meal constructed entirely of Pixie Stix and Snickers ice cream bars.

I cannot dream, because I cannot effing sleep. And I can't sleep, because there is so much to be done!

This is a common occurrence for me -- not insomnia, per se, because it is essentially self-inflicted. Despite my part in this madness, though, I don't actually want my head to be spinning...it's just that I have too many ideas tumbling around up there to let myself rest.

I am excited! I can't wait to see what the future holds. In my mind's eye, I walk through my eventual house, classroom, and community. I mull over the pros and cons of possibly selling our current house earlier than planned, smashing our debts by over half in one logistical move. I remember that I need to do a live Facebook video tomorrow -- wait, was that today? Nope, it's definitely tomorrow. ...Whew!

You can see how this type of forward-thinking cognitive wanderlust can serve as no easy foreplay for slumber. But I'm just so thankful and *pumped for my future, surely I won't miss another five minutes of sleep*

tomorrow if I juuuuust finish this one last "daydream"!

As a collegiate shot put thrower in the NCAA, I would constantly strive to reach, and subsequently conquer, my ever-growing dreams. I worked and I sweated and I sacrificed. I pushed myself so relentlessly that I honestly wanted to quit many times. I cried and I cheered and I met some of my very best friends throughout this process. And I never took my eyes off the prize, though my target became bigger with each year of eligibility. Eventually, I broke the Kansas State University all-time record and became the 2016 NCAA Division-I Indoor National Women's Shot Put Champion. I earned the opportunity to compete at the United States Olympic Trials. I chased my ambition, and I loved every moment of this journey...even the ones that I absolutely hated at the time.

All that is more than two years in the past now, and, though I cherish the experience, I am more able to focus my attention on my sense of self, my aspirations, and some other burgeoning areas of interest.

So. What, exactly, does all that mean?

Lately, I have been mulling around the idea that there might be a statute of limitations on ambition. If an idea resides exclusively in your head and is never coupled with any action, can you truly call it a "dream"? How many times can a lifelong goal be attempted and abandoned before you are forced to reckon with your own lack of motivation? These are the guilty thoughts that plague my sleepless nights...after each time I give up on writing a book. Again.

I have created and developed characters, scrawled hasty outlines on fresh, crisp notebook pages, and read sporadically in search of inspiration --

and yet, up to this point, my pains have birthed no book. *Why is this?* I have wondered, on more than a few occasions. *Why is it that a goal so important to me has slipped through my fingers countless times, even as I made plans (yet again) to achieve it?* Admittedly, I still don't have the entire answer to this question, as in athletics I never struggled with this particular obstacle. I have not yet figured out exactly why I have not, in any of my previous writing endeavors, succeeded.

I do have a couple of theories, though.

On the one hand, I believe that all significant events throughout the Universe are properly pre-sequenced insofar as we are open to them (and no malice intervenes). Therefore, I strongly feel and have witnessed that, while not everything "happens for a reason" (ugh, *hate* that phrase), great results are often born out of initial disappointment. For example, you may try and fail a hundred times to become a famous singer, only to network, grind, and hone your craft to the point that you one day find yourself a famous *songwriter* instead, selling your tunes to Lady Gaga and making *bank*.

I would most definitely NOT consider this result a failure; rather, I would encourage you to celebrate the destination you reached, just by relentlessly chasing your initial vision. In much the same way, I arrived at the scene of this book not by "quitting" on my writing...but rather, by improving my craft, gaining confidence, and abandoning stories which I do not believe would have been as enjoyable or (hopefully) as successful.

Another thought I have had is that I needed to experience more of others' writing in order to complete the vision of my first written work. I needed to try out new styles, listen to alternative ideas, and allow myself to be inspired by other (particularly *female*) writers. It was through this continual "training" that I found myself hungrier and hungrier to share my own original work.

I want to pass along to you a short list of amazing female-authored books that I have read (or experienced the audiobook for) in the past few months. I would encourage you to check them out, and (to be wildly honest), I would suggest that, even if audiobooks aren't generally your thing, you listen to the words read in the voice of the author, for an added splash of flavor. I *love* listening to funny and ambitious women "talk to me" about their lives, triumphs, embarrassments, and lessons learned.

1. *Yes, Please* by Amy Poehler
2. *Bossypants* by Tina Fey
3. *You Are a Badass: How to Stop Doubting Your Greatness and Start Living an Awesome Life* by Jen Sincero
4. *Girl, Wash Your Face* by Rachel Hollis
5. *I am Malala* by Malala Yousafzai
6. *The Last Black Unicorn* by Tiffany Haddish

In reading or listening to these books (several of which will be on my chapterly list of literary suggestions), you can catch a glimpse into the lives of women whose experiences can educate, validate, or enliven your own...and also sometimes make you laugh-shoot Cheetos out of your nose in the car.

The Choice is Mine: Finding Your Fine

When I suggest that you "find your *fine*" or "purposefully practice *fine*," I want to be crystal clear about something: when this idea for this book first came to me (probably during some sleepless night of future planning), I was not in the healthiest of emotional places. I had just begun to visit with Gina, and when she suggested the idea, maybe by accident, that Fine was to be a *goal* for me. I didn't take it as well as I wish I had.

Although I was on the uptick and doing all the right things (filling my life with positive literature, seeing a counselor, making friends at my new job), I was still feeling a little down on myself in the confidence department. "Fine" felt a little bit like giving up. It felt like a resignation to a less-than-perfect existence, something I had never even considered before, due to the deep-rooted, warped, and low sense of inherent self-worth I was merely beginning to uncover. I compiled a list of possible chapter titles for my work, but at the time, a few of them sounded something like this:

- Your boss may or may not like you.
- A change of scenery might make you feel less shitty.
- You are reasonably physically fit.
- People don't hate having conversations with you.
- I will eventually die, and I don't have a happy feeling about it.

Damn...Remember, I wasn't exactly at my sparkly, shining best.

As I continued on my journey -- practicing yoga, meditation, positive affirmation, and regular writing -- something began to shift within my psyche. Suddenly, I began to perceive Fine as a place of warmth -- an ideology, rooted in comfort, self-love, security, and true, joyful happiness. How could this emotional one-eighty appear so effortless? Well, truth be told, it took (and still, today, takes) a lot of hard, mindful work in order to maintain my positive outlook on Fine. I have to remind myself that I am worthy of love and confidence on a daily basis, through a careful combination of both regimented practice and unconditional self-forgiveness.

I am instilling the habit within myself that I need *grace* and *support*...and that these things, ultimately, must come from within. They must be organic, and they must be *instinctual*. In this way, I am learning to cultivate within my soul the love and acceptance I have so longed for -- that, in fact, I have at times lashed out for. On the flipside, I constantly remind myself that I must be diligent in my quest for habitual self-love. If I want my internal affirmation "muscles" to grow, then I need to give them a workout, even on the days when I don't feel like it.

THIS careful BALANCE is the "purposeful practice of fine," my friends.

It is the constant filling of your proverbial cup with positive, inspirational, and self-esteem-building content to the point that the dang cup *literally* overflows! It is only from a place of Fine that we can give true and free love to others, and it is the only way we will find *joy* in trying to do so. I invite you to join me on this ongoing journey toward Fine.

It has taken a long-term sense of commitment and *lots* of caffeine to make it this far into my journey of Fine. And I'm nowhere near my final destination! However, I have been on this road long enough to understand its importance, as well as my own beauty and existential value. And, through this book and my story of stumbling and ever -ripening retribution, I hope to help you to discover the same feelings within yourself.

From the first step, please know that you are the *best* kind of fine, and you are inherently worthy of love -- and, from that very secure and supportive head space, I invite you to journey forward with me.

A Book to Read or Listen to... *Bossypants* by Tina Fey

Chapter #2:
Call Yourself Beautiful, Damnit!

I raise the pencil to my face, slowly. Drawing a black line ever-so-gingerly across the waterline of my left eye, I strain not to let myself blink, lest I ruin my perfect eyeliner job.

I am in the high school bathroom, staring at myself now, in the dimly lit single mirror. Single. *Huh, that's a familiar concept, isn't it? I check my make-up one last time and then turn sideways to check out the reflection of my tummy poodge prior to rejoining my friends in the cafeteria.*

Maybe once I get boobs it won't look like my stomach sticks out so far, *I think.* Maybe then I'll finally get his attention in class...or maybe I'll talk to him on MSN Messenger again tonight. *Yeah, probably that.*

....

The concept of beauty has long eluded me, particularly as a means to accurately describe myself. In order to illustrate this disconnect, I would like to regale you with a very funny story:

Once upon a time, I was the prom queen. I was also incredibly fashionable and great at applying makeup correctly. I was reassured constantly of my fiery good looks by those around me, who were in obvious awe of my natural physique, perfect-off-the-pillow hair, dazzling smile, and small, button nose. The end.

Come now, laugh with me!

I used to be bitter about the fact that I simply wasn't, as the Maybelline commercials of my youth sang to me of "naturally" beautiful models, "...born with it." What *I* was born with is a basketball-shaped face, a precariously crooked nose, a loud, bellowing laugh, and hips set so high that my core would appear to be almost nonexistent, were it not for my inevitable and ever-present spare tire (*Ya'know? That extra little jiggle that wraps all the way around the middle?*). In short, it was not often, growing up, that another person would refer to me as anything remotely similar to "beautiful"...and, if they had, it would undoubtedly have caused me acute social discomfort. To be honest, the mere thought of someone calling me beautiful made me squirm because *I didn't believe it.*

Furthermore, after taking a magnifying glass to the insecurities of my youth, I have realized that not only did I not believe that I was beautiful on the outside, but I also didn't believe that I deserved this (or any) accolade on the *inside.* Some part of me, hidden down deep and hushed by social convention and anxiety, whispered greedily up through the channels of my heart, *You are not worthy to accept compliments. You do not deserve reassurance. You must accept your horrid plain-ness and always know that you are a lesser being.* You can imagine how this might have affected my self-confidence and ability to form healthy relational attachments, among other things.

I was wholeheartedly and woefully insecure throughout my middle- and high-school years. Since that time, I have heard many people refer to their own "Ugly Duckling" stage, while chuckling at the reminiscence of their six-month battle against acne and uneven bangs. My experience, on the other hand, ran much deeper. I distinctly remember one family photo, taken for our church directory my seventh-grade year. This was the pre-braces age of small, oval glasses, wet-looking gelled hair, and ZERO concept of eyebrow maintenance. When the picture was printed and proudly displayed in my parents' living room, I was positively mortified.

In high school, I threw myself furiously into sports. I reasoned that, if I couldn't be the prettiest girl on the team, I could at least be the loudest, strongest, and most intense player in the entire league. Even though my athletic prowess did not gain me any romantic secret admirers, at least I was getting attention...though that sometimes meant being referred to as "a man" for my strength and aggressive playing style. Sadly, even though my love for sport did not fade, it was not getting me any closer to feeling beautiful.

The issue with this logic was not that my athletic endeavors were *bad*; it was that I used this success to ignore the painful truth that I couldn't utilize the same avenues as some of my girl friends in order to gain approval. I could not, like them, tousle my beautiful curly (not-at-all-sweaty) ponytail in slow motion, while tossing my head back and windchime giggling about post-game party plans. Trust me, I tried it once, and somebody asked me with concern if I was "feeling alright?"

When it came time for school-wide dances, I tried my damnedest to look "hot" in the hopes that, if I couldn't pull off beautiful, that I could at least attract the one thing that I thought might still give me confidence: a fricken *boyfriend*. I wanted so badly for a boy to call me beautiful, and I often dreamed up some half-baked, you-and-me-against-the-world fantasy, in which the (gorgeous) guy of my dreams would reassure me that the rest of humanity had been blind all along…and that I truly was beautiful, through the lens of his love for me. (Please refrain from gagging until the end of this chapter).

When I started dating my first "real" boyfriend during my sophomore year, my romantic novelesque plan did actually work for a little while. Though I never explicitly revealed the secret of my deep-seeded need to *believe* someone who called me beautiful, he told me that I was, all the same…up until he broke up with me via text message, to get back with the ex-girlfriend he had referred to as a "psycho" during our entire, two-month-long fling (*Lordy, how many lessons can a girl learn from one experience?*). This minor flirtation with relationship-induced confidence took its fateful blow, and all was back to normal once more.

Throughout the rest of high school and on into college, my subconscious belief that a weiner pointed in my direction would somehow constitute "beauty" only intensified. It wasn't sex that I was looking for, really, but the idea that I was sexually *desirable*. You see, by this point, I had made a nasty deal with the devil in my subconscious: I would drop the whole "beauty" routine, if I could just be *wanted*, which, I reasoned (though only to myself), was what I had really been yearning for in the first place. However, there was a small problem: crippling anxiety was still brutally fucking me up.

Every time I would get close to a guy (and, therefore, my new and improved self-concept), I would be hit with an explosive-diarrhea-type panic. At the time, I blamed God for most of my break-ups, reasoning that it must not be "true love" if I was *literally* (not romantically) unable to breathe. To this day, I still believe that there was a cosmic element to my inability to form lasting relationships -- both romantic and platonic. Buuuut I also know that I used these feelings as a cop-out more than once.

Now, this isn't to say that I did not make some lifelong friends in college. Some of my very favorite people started out as classmates and fellow athletes; however, I would argue that many of them are my closest friends *in spite* of the anxiety I battled, not because I was any kind of great comrade.

I wish I could begin this next paragraph by sharing that I have solved this problem entirely. I so badly wish that I could tell you that I met and fell in love with my husband just after completely banishing anxiety from my life and embracing a self-assured beauty that I truly believed in. However, to say this would make me nothing more than a round-faced liar. The ugly truth is, I have been through absolute hell in order to achieve what flimsy sense of self-love I now continuously labor to maintain.

Truth be told, I don't know that, before writing this book, I had ever, once, referred to myself as "beautiful." I think the closest I've come was saying a quick, "I'm kind of cute," followed by the classically self-deprecating, "I guess. But not really." HOW SAD IS THAT? How am I supposed to know and recognize the beauty in the world if I cannot see it in myself and SPEAK it? This step is crucial because it would mean admitting to the world that: 1) I deem beauty to be a thing of importance, and 2) I am in awe of something that I inherently possess. I did nothing to earn it (physical beauty is given), but I can work to fan its flames by proclaiming its truth and that of my internal beauty as well. I cannot do this if I deny it or shrink my self-concept so as not to inconvenience anyone else.

In order to arrive in the whole "I *actually* think I'm beautiful" head space, it is important to first define beauty for yourself. I grew up always wanting laugh lines (or "crow's feet") because my Grandma had them, and my Grandma is beautiful. Now that I am old enough to have been socialized, I sometimes worry that my already-present laugh lines are somehow *bad*. On these days, though, my unconventionally wonderful husband reminds me that he adores them. To him, my laugh lines are memories of all the times he's made me smile. And, while I need to find this assurance within myself and my mirror, it helps to know that not everyone's standards of "beauty" are the same.

What is beauty to you? What are your favorite, most beautiful parts of yourself, and how can you remind yourself both that you possess beauty in these ways *and* that it is healthy and positive to acknowledge and even (*gasp!*) celebrate them??

Understand that your confidence and self-love are only off-putting to people who do not want to see you happy. Additionally, assuming that people find you annoying for loving yourself will only make it true. You see, if you don't believe that you are worth other people's time and attention, then you will act in ways that (*ding, ding, ding!*) lose you their time and attention!

This is another example of a self-fulfilling prophecy...it's like the saying, "Truly crazy people don't *think* they're crazy." Just the fact that you are aware of your effect on other people proves that you are not carelessly obnoxious and frustrating. However, you exhaust yourself and block your own success by assuming that your very nature and essence irritate those around you.

So...here goes! If I'm going to ask you to call yourself beautiful, I guess I'd better do the same. ...Right?

The Choice is Mine: Finding Your Fine

Let's embark on a challenge together, shall we? Look at the calendar right now. What day is it? Put a mark on the square for today, and then count out 30 days from now. Mark that square, too. From this day on, until you cross off that thirtieth day, here's what I want you to do (I'll do it, too):

Find a mirror, and stare into it. Out loud (audibly enough that, if anyone else was in the room, they would hear you) and, with a smile, say the words: "I am beautiful, and I love myself."

And that's it!

This practice is a great precursor to utilizing a longer daily list of affirmations. It is a small step that can radically change your self-esteem and mood. You are worth your *own* affection -- let that sink in!

Once you have completed this 30-Day Love-Out-Loud Challenge, tell your friends about it. Tell your sister, and your uncle, and your librarian. If you can convince them to join you, embark on a *second* thirty days, right alongside them. Continue this cycle, adding more affirmations to your list each month. And wait for your mind to be blown.

I can't wait to meet the *you* who loves *YOU*!

"I AM BEAUTIFUL, AND I LOVE MYSELF."   -- Dani Hartung, 2019

A Book to Read or Listen to... *P. Zonka Lays an Egg* by Julie Paschkis

**_Update_: I completed this resolution, which I began to refer to simply as "The Mirror Challenge," and the results were, genuinely, quite surprising. On many evenings throughout the month of January, I would go to shut off my bedroom light, only to hear my husband say, knowingly, "Wait -- have you done your challenge for tonight?" I would roll my eyes and grump my way over to the mirror, feeling awkward and undeserving. Staring sullenly at my soft tum and droopy, tired eyes, I would mumble, "I'm b'tful nd I'love m'self. *Okay?*"

It was honestly a difficult habit to get into, mostly because I was living out the old adage, *Fake it 'til you make it.* I felt a mixed bag of emotions while fakely affirming myself in this way, namely: 1) embarrassment, 2) awkwardness, 3) perceived narcissism, 4) pain, and 5) hope. It was this last feeling, the *hope* -- the hope that I might one day actually believe the words I so dreaded saying out loud -- as well as the Instagram promise I had made to complete the Mirror Challenge, that forced me to recite the words each night.

I am happy to report that, though I had to open my heart wide and dissect all of those negative emotions, wrestling the demons of my self-loathing, I have come out on the other side of the Mirror Challenge with a confidence and awareness of my own beauty that I never imagined I would find! Admittedly, this took a bit longer than 30 days (more like five-ish months and counting). And it took more habitual self-affirmation than the Mirror Challenge alone.

But, by the time I reached the point where I find myself today, it was as if the time couldn't have flown by any faster. I genuinely feel such sadness for the girl who originally started writing this chapter. She was in for such a journey.

But she was in for such sweet, sweet healing.

She was on her way toward Fine.

Chapter #3:

I'm Not Classy, I'm Dani

I am hiking on a beautiful Colorado mountainside. This is my favorite kind of day, with the warm summer wind barely blowing hard enough to rustle the tree branches, as the sun beams kiss my bare shoulders and make my cheeks glisten. I look over at my husband, Ivan, who is taking a picture of the mind-blowing sunset. My dog, Willow, pauses loyally at my side and gratefully accepts the drink of water I offer to him.

This is absolute beauty. This is amazing.

Then...this is the cacophony of me, ripping an impressive fart that interrupts the sounds of nature momentarily to relieve me of the activity-induced pressure in my gut.

Oh, yeah...this is the life.

....

Despite my mother's best efforts and a lifetime of attempted socialization, I cannot say that I qualify as what any person over the age of thirty would deem a "lady." My mom (bless her heart) bestowed upon me a lifetime's worth of lectures during my upbringing, reminding me of how these "lady" creatures are supposed to behave, saying things like, "Ladies don't belch at the table," or "Ladies don't yell 'fuck you!' at the vacuum cleaner."

I don't know whether to chalk it up to innate stubbornness, abnormally high testosterone levels, or something altogether different, but I have never wanted to magically morph into a *lady*. And it's not that I don't embrace my femininity (though this wasn't always the case). I like being a *female human being*, but I have never fancied the perceived connotation of being *ladylike*. To be a lady, in this way, is to be several things I don't want to be (*petite, quiet, classy*), as well as several things I physically *can't* be (*petite, quiet, classy*).

I am a five-foot-ten-inch Amazonian woman, with big shoulders and a 405-pound all-time deadlift max. This girl ain't dainty! I also love snort-laughing to a fault, even (especially) at my own jokes...sooo, being quiet has never been second nature for me, either. And "class" -- ahhh, the ever-elusive concept of class -- is an almost comical pursuit for this Vulga German *frau* to even attempt. Mostly, that's because my little heart's just not in it! I don't have a vested interest in conforming to a pretentious, idealistic mold.

I actually told my mom once that, if I ever found a boy who would engage with me in a belching competition, I would marry him. She shook her head, sad and slow, and said something to the effect of, "Honey, but you'll never get a husband, then." I think she may even have shed a single, glistening tear. Welp, I hated (kidding; *loved*) to break it to her, but that is my *exact* love story, Mommy Dear! Comfortable with each other's yuckiness very early on, Ivan and I quickly became thick as thieves, if thieves snarf Chinese food and talk openly about toenail clippings. *Who needs to act like a lady*, I mused, feeling mighty vindicated, *when you can eat pizza, burp and fart, and then suck face with a hottie?*

Now, in the interest of full-bodied disclosure, I would like to sheepishly admit that, in some ways, I reject the concepts of "ladylike" and "classy" due merely to my own misconceptions. I tell myself that adhering to the social expectations of the "hawt girls" will make me a stuffed shirt. A stick in the mud. A douche, if you will. And so, to be quite honest, perhaps I fear that an attempt to fit into the mold might result in my accidentally breaking it (I am quite clumsy and have a knack for breaking things that aren't even easily breakable).

I pretend that I was born into some lower socioeconomic status in the unspoken caste system of our global economy. I act as though having class somehow strips me of loyalty to my roots (which actually are relatively poor, financially-speaking). But what if I started to explore this concept with more of an open mind? Just for review, remember that I definitely still do not want to be a meek little mouse who curtsies and says, "Yes, sir," when her husband hollers for another beer with his hand down his pants and a smidge of salsa on his chin.

What I am saying, however, is that I intend to accept and love myself for boldly displaying characteristics which I like to refer to as "class-ish" or "Dani-like". I plan to be classic-with-a-twist, in my own way, and in my own time.

In my life, I have so badly wanted to make an impression that I have entirely abandoned class -- outright refusing to practice or expand my understanding of it. "Too busy to be classy" has been my mantra, because I was operating from an emotional place of *lack*. What I mean by this is that I have spent a lot of my time focused on what I didn't have (or the person that I didn't instinctually know how to be), and that mindset created a habit in which I thought, "Why try harder? Acting classy won't change my situation." But I am learning that cutting these corners won't work over time, especially when one begins to develop substantial, long-term dreams.

Growing up, all my needs were met, and my parents did an amazing job of sacrificing and scraping so that my sisters and I would never have to go without. That said, there was always this sinking fear, this hungry elephant in the room. There was always debt. There were always bills to pay, that came due too quickly -- and paychecks that were too few and far between. As hard as they worked to maintain the facade, my parents couldn't entirely conceal their financial strain. From a very early age, I knew that money was not something we had an abundance of.

I suppose, at that time, it seemed like "class" was linked exclusively to monetary wealth. It seemed as though some people didn't share my worries about money, and they were, therefore, freer to study and become experts in the ways of classy behavior. It wasn't until recently that I began to mold and re-make my understanding of class, using a much less formal method.

The truth is that *class*, in some ways, just means *love*. To behave with class means to respect the sensibilities of others, even as you chase your own ambition and self-interest. You can rise to transform into your most accomplished self (finding success, notoriety, money, and friendship, if those are things that will bring you happiness). The crazy thing is, you can do this while simultaneously pulling others upward *with* you, and treating them with respect and patience along the way (read: classy).

Sometimes, class looks like my dad, who worked multiple part-time jobs in addition to his full-time teaching position and coaching supplementals.

Sometimes, it looks like my mom, shushing her daughters and telling them that money troubles were no concern of theirs -- that their job was simply to "be kids." And sometimes, it looks like my coach and most honored mentor, Norma, who taught me, always, that, "It's not where you start that matters; it's where you finish."

In short, class is both a state of mind and a consistent demonstration of respect and love for others. It's not about wealth, in the financial sense. It's about *you*. Who you *are* as a person. And you simply can't operate from that animalistic place of lack if you want to have any hope of treating others with genuine, selfless class.

The Choice is Mine: Finding Your Fine

If you struggle, like me, with the predisposed notion that you are not, and will never be, considered "classy," take a moment to assess the roots of this assumption. Do you plan to live a sweats-and-messy-bun life for the rest of your days *purely* out of the fear that others might judge your attempts to appear *debonaire*, or does it *truly* make you feel empowered? Do you want something different -- something (slightly) classier?

To come to terms with the fact that I can be quirky *and* class-ish, I need to accept myself for the Fine, deserving person that I am. I have to remind myself that class doesn't equate to pretense of perfection, or haughty lordliness. (In fact, people like this are often the *least* classy.) Rather, if I view class as a flexible state of being, in which I strive not to be fake, but to be the most genuine version of myself, then I am much more motivated to pursue a classy way of life.

I will use my unique attributes as assets in my journey toward class-ishness. I will work to make others feel supported and capable and worry-free. I will treat people with respect, even when it is inconvenient to do so, pulling them upward as much as they'll let me. Once I have readjusted my mindset surrounding my ability to be classy, I will be able to pour out this confidence and love into the lives of others.

I will use self-affirmation to remind myself that I have nothing to fear. I will confidently display class as a means of communicating love and empathetic respect. I will not use obnoxious indifference as a deflection of my previous assumption that I couldn't "afford" to be classy. I will strive to emulate class in my everyday life. But let's not be fake, friend. In the comfort of my own home? I'm still belching at the table.

A Book to Read or Listen to... *Yes, Please* by Amy Poehler

Chapter #4:

An Ode to Typos

My typos, they are friends of mine
Who sneak and condescend
Sometimes they go unnoticed, But
Their goal is to upend

I've always hated typos,
Yet now I've come to see
That I am only human when
I accidentally...

Fuck up. The Edn.

....

Ahhh, the "professional email". How I hate thee.

Why do I feel such heated disdain for something so trivial? So routine? The truth is, I am initially mortified at the thought of any form of written communication which can be recorded, traced, and held against me in a court of law. I have always been hyper-aware of the impact born from what lives *between* the lines of text (intentional or not), and I am made equally uncomfortable by the possibility that someone on the receiving end of an irrevocably marred sentence might consider me rude, unintelligent, or worse -- *lazy*.

Think about it. How many times have you heard someone snicker over an incoherent Facebook status, or chortled around the water cooler about that time when Barb from Accounting accidentally forwarded her nasty gossip to the whole division, instead of just to Ted? How about that time when you unknowingly sent a text to a fresh significant other, saying something like, "Wanna suck a movie later?" *Damn autocorrect.*

In my little busy-bee, bumbling brain, the list of potentially horrifying mess-ups is infinite. Each day that goes by, each Instagram comment, and each staff report is a golden opportunity to make an ass of myself. Granted, situations like this literally *have* happened to me. In high school, I got caught red-handed, and more than once, spewing unkind drivel about my rivals and friends. I have sent a sneaky text to the wrong person. I have submitted collegiate essays (*that I proofread a* hundred *times!*) to my professors, wrought with misspellings and embarrassingly low levels of creative organization. I have been unable to extract the entire word I wished to use from my brain, straining for an uncomfortable amount of time to vomit the sucker out of my mouth...usually in front of somebody important.

I think that part of this seeming overreaction to *typos*, and other things of the sort, stems from my overall insecurity as a young, female professional. I try to write the perfect email so that my boss won't see that I accidentally wore shoes I'm not too sure about. I obsess over my social media accounts, watching and re-watching my video posts to make sure that no one can see me slouching or hear me say, "Um," too many times. I secretly and silently rehearse what I plan to say on the phone before I place any work calls, so that I can sound witty and smart and friendly...that way, whomever is on the other end of the line won't know that I am suuuuper nervous about the professionalism of the bright, new lip color I am rocking today. This works great! If I keep up the facade 100% of the time, then they'll never see what I'm missing, right?

The issue now has become that all of this effort, emotional energy, and self-deprecation has become...EXHAUSTING.

I spend entire shifts in a self-created no-man's land, somewhere between "eggshells" and "pins and needles." I jump, startled at the sound of my ringing phone, and have to take a quick belly breath before I can bring myself to answer it with the chipper, laughing tone I wish to perform. I read, read, and re-read emails before I hit "send," and sometimes I even go *back* and read them again, after the fact! And any time that I try to cut loose, try to advocate for my mental health against the siege of self...I feel lazy, incompetent, and vulnerable. And so, the battle wages on.

A big part of my current job is a heaping pile of public speaking, which I love! When I am in front of a group of people, particularly when I am well-prepared, I am on top of the world. Words come to me quickly, I utilize the space around me to make my audience feel relaxed and attentive, and time seems to stand still. However, it never fails that, the moment the clapping ends and I come down from the high, I can instantly spot about one-hundred aspects of the presentation that could have been improved.

Just today, I called a friend and co-worker while driving away from a presentation in a high school counselor's office. "Is it just me," I asked, "or will I just, literally, *never* be satisfied with any presentation I give? Like, I seem to remember a new tidbit each time that I made a note to mention...but I *always* forget something else!" I don't mean to be a Negative Nance here, but Jiminy Christmas! It's frustrating when you are trying to be hella impressive but also constantly leave speaking engagements feeling like you just handed them something much like lukewarm oatmeal with a soft smile and no spoon. You know, something that's nice (enough) but just not satisfying!

So, if you add this post-presentation anxiety to the worrisome concepts of typos, stutters, dress code, and boardroom etiquette, you can pretty accurately describe my work brain as an incessant echo chamber of spiraling shame and dorkiness (but nothing too dramatic, though). How am I supposed to go from *that* to Fine??

What can I do to combat this neurotic overcompensation which, in the end, actually defeats its own purpose by *wasting* time? I set out to compile a list of to-do's to help me improve my work performance and sense of professional confidence as a young up-and-coming. I'm still far from an expert, but here's what I've come up with so far:

1. Get yourself a ride-or-die

When you're in the throes of self-doubt and panicked frustration, you will need some level-headed support and empathetic validation. This is where work friends come in. In fact, according to Cosmopolitan magazine[1], the ability to befriend and cooperate with co-workers can make or break your career. In their words, "Having a work wife makes you better at your job."

It is incredibly beneficial to go to someone who is either a.) simultaneously struggling with the same issues and insecurities that you are, or b.) recently graduated from your level of development and therefore operating

---

[1] "Having a work wife makes you more productive, study says" by Lucy Wood (February 6, 2018). https://www.cosmopolitan.com/uk/worklife/news/a49662/work-friends-key-to-career-success/

from an elevated perspective. In fact, the best method I've come across is to have *both* of these types of friends at work. You will find yourself in cahoots with the girl who started in the office the same week as you, while also being advised by your steadfast and experienced mentor. In the world of work spouses, polygamy is key! The only caveat to this is that all of your co-workin' warriors need to be positive, uplifting, and useful in their advice and affirmations. No Johnny Rainclouds for you! The temptation to display one's organizational knowledge in the form of constant criticism will be palpable as you rise through the ranks. Don't allow yourself to fall into this trap with co-workers who poo on everyone else's positivity. Go back to your partners in crime and soak up their awesomeness!

2. Sanity over Productivity

It can be so tempting to work through lunch or stay late when you're on a roll, or take your laptop home every night to "just finish what you started." I am here to tell you, this is no way to live! One of my most eye-opening personal revelations is that I do not have a motivation problem; while many people need someone to coax and coach and fire them up, I am harder on myself than any sergeant-major could be. I, on the other hand, actually need someone to periodically remind me to *relax*.

Some days, this looks like grabbing anyone in close proximity for a chatty walk through the crisp, fall air over to Starbucks. Other days, it means not talking to *anyone*, and closing your door for a solid ten-minute meditation (pro tip: you may need to turn off the lights and crawl beneath your desk to create the illusion that you are not, in fact, in your office).

Also, don't discount the effectiveness of the world-famous (yet often misunderstood) Mental Health Day. It is A-OK to call in "sick" or even simply work from home every now and again if you are feeling overwhelmed and disconnected. This refreshing experience can give you the boost you need to be productive and pleasant for the rest of the week!

3. Leave Work at Work

Try not to bring your frustrations from work home to your friends or significant other. Take any time necessary to disconnect from your worries before walking through your front door. If it helps you, make this "shedding site" a specific time and place on your way home every single day. For me, I work toward full-fledged belly breaths on my homebound commute, so that any work-related woes can be left in the car (side note: I'm still working on this practice, as my wonderfully patient husband can attest).

The Choice is Mine: Finding Your Fine

Recently, I watched a video online about what is known as "Imposter Syndrome". Individuals who battle Imposter Syndrome, even when they are actually doing a great job, constantly feel like they are "fooling" everyone into *thinking* that they are doing awesomely, when, in reality, they don't believe that they are. This is a frustrating mindset, which I have had to fight against in the professional sphere. I live in the constant, nagging fear that my peers and superiors will one day find out that I am a fraud -- that I am truly nothing more than a chump who simply wandered in one day and has been bullshitting for a paycheck ever since.

If you struggle with feelings of secret incompetence, let me be the first to grab you by the face and let you know: it ain't true! You are doing your best, which is already an *amazing* job! On top of that, you are learning and improving and networking, all of which are helping you to morph into one badass (legitimate) professional.

Our first job, together, is to combat these insecurities by redefining "professionalism" for the Millennial audience. The traditionalist views of professionalism are 1) about as outdated as a "no visible tattoo" rule and 2) absolute fairy tale horse shit.

Some of this fantasy stems from a patriarchal and prejudiced system, which has been stuck in the fifties for ages now. The thing is, in my experience, the concept of professionalism is *far* more fluid if you are a man's man a business degree, though I have met (and been mentored by) some admirable men who recognize and are equally frustrated by this disparity. Unfortunately, having them in my corner does not an equitable society make. In many organizations today, what is acceptable in terms of language, expectations, and literacy is not necessarily required, so long as you're a "sharp-dressed man."

Now, perhaps this is not your experience! I would encourage you, though, whether you are a man or a woman, to start some open and frank (probably off-the-clock) discussions with co-workers of both sexes. Ask them questions about how they perceive professionalism, Imposter Syndrome, and general workplace acceptance -- and see who is more likely to experience professional anxiety. How do they feel about the intersectionality of gender stereotypes (or other facets of marginalization) in any of these categories?

40

We are beyond the question of, "Why are women in the workplace?" This sentiment is honestly a gross piece of our history, and it's, sadly, not entirely eradicated in the present day. To be honest (and let me say this slowly and clearly for the grouches in the back): WOMEN CAN DO WHATEVER THEY WANT. You want to work within the home, raising beautiful children? That's wonderful! You'd rather have an illustrious career in the professional sphere? You go, too, girl! Unfortunately, it is not generally *completely* acceptable to choose either of these trajectories. For the time being, let's bring our focus back to the workplace.

As women, it is not our job to sit idly by and allow unfairly skewed and rigid standards to continue. And the task of changing it, darlin', falls squarely on us! Work to build up other professional women (and all other individuals suffering from professional marginalization), speak out against the "bitchy boss" stereotype, and pay attention to wage inequality, even if you never have before. Take ownership of your own professionalism, and you might be shocked to find that your confidence skyrockets, right along with your feelings of empowerment and belonging.

Affirm yourself, literally, *at* work. At your desk, in your office, in the lobby...put your shoulders back, smile, speak loudly, and shake hands *hard*. You are a frickin' boss. Speak that truth to yourself in the bathroom mirror. Say it aloud to other women at your job. Utilize the proper channels if you need to report injustice, and do not back down.

A lot of workplace insecurity, for me, stemmed from feelings that I did not belong there. I was the "new girl" and I didn't want to make waves. You know what? That kind of thinking isn't going to get us anywhere. You might trip and fall. You might have a stain on your shirt, or forget someone's name. You might send out a typo to the whole department, and guess what?

EVEN THEN,

You are awesome! You are competent! You are a leader!

YOU are FINE.

A Book to Read or Listen to... *The Last Black Unicorn* by Tiffany Haddish

Chapter #5:

Namaste: An Ongoing Experience of Fitness

Inhale.

Downward dog position, trying to connect to my breath. Meanwhile, my actual dog is panting heavily in the background.

Exhale.

Fuck, I really need to do laundry. And I forgot to text Emi back. Shit. Okay, hold on. Reconnecting to my breath (again), setting my intention for today's yoga practice. Focus. I am worthy of taking this time for myself.

Inhale.

This is about me. This is good for my body. This is healthy for my mind. "Damnit! Baaaaaabe, can you get the lasagna out of the oven?" *Shit, okay. Back to my breath. Here we go.*

Exhale.

Plank position. Vinyasa. I like myself.

Inhale.

Upward-facing dog. Create space. I love myself.

Exhale.

Downward dog. Walk out the legs. Stretch the calves. This is for me. Breathe. Practice. Love.

....

On the road working as a collegiate admissions recruiter, I find that I am in both the best and worst position to better my physical fitness. On the one hand, I have lots of time to myself and frequent access to hotel fitness centers boasting at least one functional treadmill. On top of this, I have wifi-enabled Internet access, placing at my fingertips the power to find videos of any type of exercise I could imagine.

And then, of course, there's the other hand.

I'm freakin' *tired*! Aaalllllllll the time, dude. This week, for example, I participated in an on-campus bus trip (which, translated, means that I was at work at 5:00 pm on Sunday night, spent that night sleeping on an air mattress in a gym full of prospective students, and then woke up the next morning at 6:00 am to traipse my happy ass all over campus, giving tours and smiles and summer camp memories). The next day, Tuesday, I worked from 8:00 am until about 4:00 pm, at which time I made the three-hour drive to the hotel in my recruiting territory. For the next two days, I stationed out of said hotel and visited four different high schools, each of which were 30- to 60-minute commutes apart.

And then, when I mercifully arrived back at my hotel room, spiritually broken, longing for a bubble bath and smelling of hand sanitizer and the tuna I spilled on myself at lunch...my whore of an Apple Watch buzzed on my wrist and jeered, "Umm, honey? You need to check your rings, girl."

In other words...some nights I'm not, like, real jazzed about breaking a sweat and burning some midnight cals. However, the beauty of this reluctance to exercise makes me feel even better when I pick my ass up off the pillowtop and do it! This evening, I was feeling both slightly creative and particularly anti-social, so I snuck down the stairs to swipe the hotel's fitness room yoga mat. (It should be noted here that I have strategically figured out which wing of the hotel I must use to take the stairs directly to the fitness center without passing through the people-filled lobby.)

I brought that bad boy up to my room and pulled up a *Yoga By Candace* video on YouTube. In the small, tiled area in front of my door and next to the bathroom, I vinyasa'd so damn hard for an hour. I knew that it was what my body needed, because I have been incredibly tight and sore from walking back and forth on campus, followed by sitting in the car for extended periods of time. I made a concerted effort to meditatively connect with the Universe, and I pondered the intention of my practice (*"To Be Rich and Awesome,"* complete with vivid images of debt-free fabulousness, to be exact).

But the most interesting aspect of this workout, besides the fact that I couldn't stop staring at Candace's ripped abs, was that, in the large, full-length mirror right next to where I'd laid my mat...I couldn't stop staring at *myself*. Let me qualify this statement by sharing that this is absolutely *not* a normal occurrence for me. I'm definitely not the poster child for a positive body image (I still, regrettably, ask my husband e-ver-y day if I'm "faaaaaat?"), but I am trying to change my perspective because I *want* to love myself completely, inside and out!

And it seems that, on this mystical October evening, I have, at this point, for the brief duration of a yoga practice, glimpsed what it must be like to love one's own body. Not just to think it's "not bad" or "okay," but to think it looks *awesome.* I tried to focus on my breathing, but I just kept watching my own physique, both impressed by its power and in tender awe of my loving connection to it. *Look at what I can do!* I thought. *Check out my moves, my muscles, and my healthier BMI resulting from a cleaner diet!* I looked at my body with a pride I haven't experienced since high school. How I would feel about myself the next morning was momentarily irrelevant, as I left feelings of vanity behind and made *uddiyana bandha* my beautiful body's bitch.

In high school (sophomore year, to be exact), I discovered that I possessed a mysterious secret which, up until that point, had been entirely hidden during my bookish and chubby pre-teen years: I was…athletic! Once I realized this about myself, and when I came to understand just how much I enjoyed both physical activity and competition, I decided that I didn't want to be known as a good basketball player, volleyball player, or shot put thrower. I wanted to be known as a great *athlete*, overall and across the board.

That was the standard to which I held myself from that point on, and whatever the price for this goal became, I made my body cash the check without hesitation. I set about utilizing my body as a tool to compete with the best of the best, no matter *what* game I was playing…and I was going to *win*.

As a collegiate shot put thrower, I had the athletic time of my life, truly competing against some of the best athletes in the nation and world. But the whole damn time, I knew that, even though I was stronger and more powerful than I'd ever been, I wasn't considered by the general population to be a good *athlete*. Shot putters on this level (at least collegiately) are not always expected to be "healthy." Rather, we are simply told to "get big" because "mass moves mass," and stocky, muscular bodies have an advantage in our sport. To make matters worse, most of the runners and multi-eventers around me judged workouts solely on the amount of running they entailed (for me, this was pretty exclusively none). So, even though I was quick on my feet and could lift a brick house, I was so far out of cardio-shape that it was laughable, and my vertical jump height could have been equated to that of a basset hound with a sumo wrestler standing on its ears. My friends, no amount of medals, records, or accolades could make me forget for very long that I was *not* in love with my body.

When my throwing career was over, I guess I just sort of thought that the weight would fall off naturally -- and quickly. However, it's kind of hard to lose weight when you're suddenly not working out for three hours a day but still eating Chinese food multiple times in a week. Also, of course, right about the time I stopped throwing, my metabolism began to slow as I rapidly approached my mid-twenties. To make matters EVEN worse, I had no concept of a healthful or sustainable diet selection. My brain said, "Eat more colorful foods, more veggies, and more whole grains!"...and my stomach said, "ME WANT WHATABURGER".

Talk about a you-versus-you game of Tug O' War.

As the months stretched into years after I officially retired from throwing (due to a hip injury I had sustained in college and never fully recovered from), I went through a roller coaster of weight loss and gain. During my lowest emotional lows, I lost massive amounts of weight simply because my anxiety gnawed away any whisper of an appetite. Then, as I got mentally healthier, I struggled with my confidence in a new way, as the pounds started to slowly creep their way back onto my midsection.

I tried a nutrition tracker app, just long enough to teach myself about healthy balance and portions, which worked wonders (as long as I paid attention to my caloric intake, I was losing weight again!). But, not wanting to be tethered to this app for my whole life and determined to test the waters for myself, I embarked on yet another up-and-down journey, as I independently wrestled my deep-rooted habits against my newly educated practices. I would try my best to keep to the lessons I had learned while using the tracker, but portion control is undeniably more difficult to stick to when you don't actually have to record what you've eaten.

And that battlefield, in essence, is where I am still. I am wrestling. I make poor decisions, I drink too many margaritas, I sometimes eat the shit out of white bread...but then, I also go running with my friends, or utilize my hotel's dumbbells and stationary bike, or drag a random yoga mat up to the third floor to join Candace for a little active rest. I *try*, damnit. I will not be a slave to calories, and I will not feel guilty for getting my money's worth at the HuHot Mongolian Grill buffet. But I will also not sit on my ass after a day's worth of driving and making college presentations to high school students who are sometimes awesome but sometimes look at me like my slow, agonizing death would bring them joy.

I will *use* this body of mine! I will move it and strengthen it and feed it and love it so, so much. We have been through hell together, this body and me. It has seen me through a period of semi-starvation at the age of 14, when I didn't think my boyfriend would continue to like me unless I was skinnier. It has felt me laugh my ass off with my friends, in our freshmen dorm eating Double-Stuff Oreos dipped in Nutella. It has seen me shaking with anxiety in the bedroom of my first apartment, sobbing with self-hatred as I called my boss to try and explain why I couldn't work my three-hour shift. And it has carried me through the toughest and most grueling workouts and competitions I could have ever imagined. It was with me as I discovered my sexuality and explored the things my body could do that we never learned about in school. It has walked me to and through new cities, jobs, and life changes. And still, here we are.

During that time in high school, right after I discovered that I was worth a shit at sports, I fell madly in love with the game of basketball. It was relatively new to me (I had previously attempted to play in middle school and was mortifyingly bad). So, with a chip on my shoulder and a fascination for the sport of it, I threw myself into high school basketball with feverish intensity. Often, I had to ask my teammates, literally mid-play, for clarification on a rule or explanation for an official's call; they had all been playing much longer than I had. But this was what I loved most about the game: there was *always* going to be something new and exciting to learn.

Even the very best basketball players in the whole world, I reasoned, could always learn a new play, a new trick shot, or a new conditioning exercise or drill to give them a fresh edge against the competition. I could play basketball for the rest of my life and never fully reach my absolute potential, but it was the pursuit of this unattainable perfection that stole my heart and passion.

Now, don't get me wrong. An equally catalytic factor in my youthful obsession with basketball was that I was (am) naturally and passionately competitive. I wanted to lift the most weight, run the fastest, jump the highest, and, usually, yell the loudest in comparison to anyone else. This tendency gave my performance an edge, but it also went unchecked for years in defining my relationship with my body.

The problem?

My *only* experience with exercise was in direct relation to win-or-lose competition with others. Therefore, it was (and sometimes still is) difficult for me to match my mental intensity appropriately to the form of physical activity at hand. For example, a softball tournament is competitive. A yoga class is *not* competitive. My knee-jerk reaction in both of these scenarios, however, is to focus on being "better" than those around me...when I should be focusing on making my*self* better. The *love* for myself better.

In high school, I caught a glimpse of this truth. I had the spirit of a young grasshopper who only wanted to mold herself into the best possible athlete she could become. I was a willing pupil, often staying after practice and asking coaches for honest critiques of my skills so that I could focus on improving them. I would work out on my own in addition to the prescribed regimen of my team. I toiled away, learning plays and moves and regulations that would allow me to play better basketball on game day.

At that time, I didn't find such a complex undertaking to be intimidating or insurmountable. Quite the opposite, I threw myself into the intricate dance of this game, probably even to a fault. I was so emotionally invested in the competition that I would often cry after every game, regardless of the outcome, just as a release of pent-up energy. But despite this, I loved every single minute of the anguish, the triumph, and the camaraderie. There was no feasible "end" to the journey of learning basketball, and I found this concept delicious.

Why, then, did I begin, at some point in my young adulthood, to view weight loss, nutrition, and fitness as a pass/fail exam, rather than an ever-growing journey, like basketball? Each day, I would wake up with my impossible rubric in hand, and trudge to the mirror. *Pudgy middle?* You gave up a three-point shot. *Ate two cupcakes last night?* Missed a free throw. *Haven't worked out in three days?* Your ass got stuffed. *Final score?* Self-Loathing: 100, Dani: 0. And so it was, every, single day.

But...hello?? Why was I doing this to myself? Why was I constantly putting myself down in comparison to some unattainable idea? What was I gaining by viewing my fitness and physique as total and inevitable losses? I should have been approaching my "Best Self" in much the same way I did the *real* game of basketball!

Something that has helped me immensely in the quest to make my relationship with athletics more body-positive is the sustained and honest practice of yoga. In particular, I have become obsessed with what I call my "YouTube Yoga Practice," in which I use my husband's Playstation to cast videos onto my living room TV. From there, I spread out my mat and *Namaste* without ever leaving the house!

My favorite YouTube Yoga channel is Yoga With Adriene, by Adriene Mishler. I am continually captivated by her ability to remind me that yoga *is* fitness, but not *more* than it is wellness, both mental and emotional. These reminders, as well as her genuine encouragement to love myself, always come at just the right moments during my practice, and I am grateful for the way that yoga has been reframed in my mind over the course of this regular practice.

Today, I am still working to correct my destructive habits of allowing all physical activity to trigger a competitive response in my mind. This is not a healthy mindset to be in if my end goal is to both improve and love my body. I do not wish to associate fitness with hierarchy, but I also know that preventing this mindset can be easier said than done in today's age of Instagram, CrossFit, and plastic surgery. I am inundated on a daily basis with "ideals" that I feel pressured to attain. I don't want to admit that the personal trainer on my newsfeed is in better shape than me (even though her whole daily *job* is to work out), because I want to *win*. I want to be the *best*.

The Choice is Mine: Finding Your Fine

I know, though, that in order to operate from a place of Fine, I need to utilize yoga as a tool for mental wellness, with the secondary benefit of physical fitness. It is not an implement with which I compete against others; in fact, yoga encourages collaboration and harmony.

How can you take care of your body and mind at the same time? I would highly recommend yoga, but you might prefer a walk in the park. In any case, do what makes you feel *emotionally* fit (with the added benefit of physical activity), and you will be amazed by the way you see you yourself.

**_Update_: Since writing the original manuscript for this book, I have continued on my journey of genuine self-love. The first -- and most impactful -- lesson that I have learned hence is that truly loving one's own physical form is not a narcissistic or selfish task. Rather, in order to love others from a place of security (a place of *Fine*, if you will), I need to love my*self* and heal my heart from decades of deprecation and criticism.

I needed to remind myself that I am worthy, simply by virtue of my very existence. I am beautiful, even on the days I wake up hungover and haven't brushed my teeth. I am strong, even when I haven't lifted weights in two weeks. All of these things are Fine parts of who I am. I cannot put limitations on my own worthiness, or conditions on the love I show myself. I gain nothing from berating my own body as "less than." Rather, I only succeed in setting myself back, to interact with the world from a place of fear and lack. This is no way to live, and it quickly leads to toxicity!

I am happily learning to love my whole, entire self -- including my body, and even (especially) on days when I'm bloated and my eyebrows need a pluck. On these days, I need my own love more than ever. So, I have committed to checking myself out in the mirror more often, and giving a little *ooh, la la!* Seriously, have you ever tried it? Cat call to yourself more often, and you may find that you need the validation of others less and less with each passing day.

In all seriousness, the point I'm trying to make here is that you cannot (canNOT) love yourself...if you don't love your *whole* self. And this includes your body, right where it is and what it looks like, in this very moment in time. Not how you hope to look after your next diet. Not how you'll feel after you run the next mile. Right this very second, today. And every day of your life. Start to love the human that you are, both inside and out! Otherwise, there is no Fine, and there is no complete Moratorium.

A Book to Read or Listen to... *Leading with the Heart* by Mike Krzyzewski

Chapter #6:

Lessons in Cosmic Turnabout

TRIGGER WARNING: This chapter discusses content which may cause emotional triggers in its readers. If this text causes you to experience negative flashbacks or emotion, please promptly throw it across the room as hard as you can...and then, when you're ready, skip to the next chapter.

I want to begin this chapter by making something perfectly clear: If you, at any time, experience suicidal thoughts, PLEASE call this number: 1-800-273-8255.

You are wanted. You are loved. You matter. You are worthy of this life, and the world would NOT be a better place if you left us.

At a time not so far in the past, my thoughts on this subject were very different. *How selfish*, I thought, *that someone would choose to take their own life, instead of figuring out what was wrong or asking for help. What a cop-out! I mean, I'm sad for their family and stuff, but really? They couldn't have even* tried?

Wow, Past Dani. How insightful.

I know now that this type of thinking is privileged and clearly lacking in empathy. I have a much better perspective at this point in my life, I hope, on how to help a friend who is suffering from this type of affliction -- of feeling that they are not worthy. However, that didn't stop me from being a real dick in the past. In fact, it is partly *because* of how ignorant I was once, that I can now look at this issue with more helpful and realistic eyes.

By the time I graduated from college, I was engaged and had been living in the house my then-fiance's parents had been renting to him and his friends for a couple of years. It was me and the boys. A regular old sausage party, plus one. I absolutely loved this experience, for the most part. However, with Ivan and I freshly bachelor's degree-d and prepping to plan a wedding, we decided that we would rather foot the rent ourselves and live roommate-free for a while.

Two of our three roommates were perfectly fine with this arrangement and made plans to move out in the summer of 2016. The third, Gage, was not so keen on the idea. In fact, Gage had not been keen on much of anything for (at least) the past three years or so.

When I first came into the picture as Ivan's teammate, and then girlfriend, Gage and I became fast and close pals. I could talk to him about anything, and I wanted him to feel the same way toward me. He was one of Ivan's very first friends; the two of them shared that kind of *Sandlot* camaraderie between boys that starts in elementary school and seems like it will never end. Then, when I came along, it looked as though the three of us were all set up for a life of always having one another to lean on.

But then...Gage's behavior began to change.

He rarely wanted to do anything that involved leaving the house. In fact, going to class (if he went to class at all) was sometimes the only thing he actively *did* all day, until one of us returned home from work or practice. Then, he began to act aggressively and erratically, sometimes being in a great, gentle mood...and other times wordlessly slamming his bedroom door to be left alone, particularly when one of the rest of us brought home a guest. We embarked on a great, vicious cycle of emotion with Gage. He would be moody and short-tempered for weeks, then one day come downstairs to our room for a forty-five minute apology and conversation about why, exactly, he'd acted that way.

He never had a satisfying answer, just a heartfelt, well thought-out apology, accompanied by the declaration that we were his best friends in the world and that he would never be rude to us again. And then, a few days or weeks later, we'd be right back to square one. It got to the point that we felt like we needed to walk on eggshells in our own home; his mood seemed to dictate the entire emotional climate of the house.

We pleaded with Gage to see a therapist, to get to the bottom of why he didn't want to finish school...why he refused to get a job, despite his crippling student debt...why he felt that he needed to take his unnamed, mysterious anger out on us, if he loved us so much. We offered to go *with* him to therapy, if he would just agree to try it. He would not.

Admittedly, part of the problem was the very nature of my presence in Ivan's life. As his fiance, I was positioned in such a way that Gage felt threatened in their friendship, despite his bond with me. Mostly, he didn't want *either* of us to abandon him after graduation and our approaching wedding. We assured him that, of course, we wouldn't...but, truth be told, we were growing rapidly more wary, considering the way we were being treated and the constant shirking of our offers to help. We were frustrated and tired of the cycle, and,

57

yes, we wanted some privacy as a couple. What we meant was that we wanted physical separation and a little emotional space, though -- not an end to the friendship.

When we asked Gage to move out (either into an apartment, or into his mother's house, located just outside of town), he lost it a little bit further. Slowly, we started to find odd and disturbing "bread crumbs" around the house. First, the trash bin was dented in on the side (we found out later that he had punched it in a fit of anger). Next, we found a conspicuously placed, blood-soaked paper towel on the garage floor. After that (and worst of all), we noticed a knife, small but sharp, balanced carefully on the edge of his truck bed, in plain sight, as it was parked in the garage.

We also began to note some new and even more alarming behavior in Gage. Although it was summertime and incredibly hot, Ivan remarked that we should keep an eye on him, because he was still constantly wearing long-sleeved shirts. Eventually, we and another one of our roommates confronted Gage about this oddity in particular, and he confessed that he had been self-harming by cutting his arms with a razor blade. We told him that he needed to get help and assured him that we would support him, but when he asked me to help wrap his arms in gauze to protect his healing wounds, all the air left my body, and I froze.

It was a terrifying sight, and it rattled us badly. We locked our door when we slept that night, maybe partly because we were simply shaken, but mostly because we now knew that Gage was both violently angry and willing to cause harm as a result of this anger. We had no idea whether this could translate into an attempt to harm *us*, but we decided not to take the chance.

The next day, the world erupted. We went to my in-laws' house and told Ivan's mom everything. Before we knew it, she was on the phone with Gage's mom, with me crying in the kitchen and Ivan chiming in nervously behind me while the two women exchanged frantic versions of a story that could only end one way: Gage had to move out, immediately.

We offered every assurance that we still cared about him, but we refused to 1) live in a house with him while he was this unstable; or 2) leave him at home unattended, when he clearly needed familial oversight. Over the next several months, a blur of nastiness threatened to overtake our lives. Gage's mom sent us accusatory Facebook messages, while we tried to gently but firmly create protective boundaries around ourselves when Gage would reach out via text or email.

But in the end, we eventually left his life, reasoning that it was best for everyone.

....

Fast forward to about a year later, when Ivan and I were still in the midst of our engagement…but things weren't going so well. We were not in a good place in our relationship, and I was feeling isolated, anxious, and depressed. Ivan had made friends who felt both free to exclude me and entitled to disrespect our relationship. I sat through countless hours of anxiety attacks, hidden in public view, while these individuals drank to belligerence, sent him inappropriate (and sometimes secret) messages, and made jokes, in my presence, often about topics like having sex with him (even after being asked to stop).

The sad thing was, this whole time I wanted desperately to be friends with these people! But, when I tried to spend time with them or attempted to start a dialogue, they would often make excuses or just outright ignore me. Many nights, for me, were spent "on read" after attempting to send funny messages and memes to members of this group. Meanwhile (and simultaneously), they would send picture after incessant picture to Ivan, especially when he was supposed to be spending time with me.

I want to take a moment here to clarify that Ivan has, at this point, entirely cut off contact with these individuals and has apologized many genuine times to me for allowing and partaking in this behavior, which caused me so much humiliation and pain. I want it to be known that I do not blame him for my former feelings of self-loathing and that I appreciate greatly the subsequent work he did to regain my trust and actively help to rebuild my confidence.

At that time, though, I sank low...lower than I ever had before, or ever thought possible. I didn't happen overnight, or over the course of a few days or weeks. It was month after month of being treated like shit, combined with an anxious disposition and deep-seeded craving for acceptance that sent me spiraling into a dark place of self-hatred and a total rejection of my existential value. Add to all of this that I was in the throes of my doctor's insurance company-coerced experiment, taking anti-seizure drugs to prevent migraines, and you had a real-life recipe for disaster.

First, it was just a little thought:

Maybe I should just die.

Not "kill myself", but...*disappear. I just wish I could fade away and disappear.*

Eventually, slowly, this thought grew into an obsession that overtook my life and my every waking thought. I was so anxious that I lost any semblance of appetite, to the point that a co-worker commented that I looked "really skinny" in a tone that conveyed more concern than compliment. I felt sick to my stomach, constantly. I daydreamed incessantly -- at work, in the middle of conversations, every time I would crawl into my bed to cry -- about how and when I should Just. End. It.

Just go away, just disappear and allow everyone to live the lives it seemed so obvious to me that they truly wanted: Dani-free.

Some part of me, somewhere deep down, was still fighting, though. I didn't want to die, or at least I wanted to try one final time to see if anyone around me would object to the idea. But I was terrified to tell Ivan what I'd been thinking, because I didn't want him to feel manipulated into staying with me. I'd heard of people who threaten to commit suicide if their significant others leave them. I've never been one for begging, so that option was even more humiliating than the "dark thoughts" themselves.

Eventually, I caved. It came spilling out of me in a ghastly wail, that I'd been thinking, every moment for weeks and weeks, about my earnest wish to die. I screamed at Ivan that I needed help, that I needed to talk to someone...and that he needed to choose between me and these "friends".

It wasn't the end of my battle. Certainly, it was the very beginning of an uphill fight for my newfound self-concept and sense of inherent worth. However, in that moment, Ivan gathered me into a huge bear hug, told me that he loved me, and offered to go with me to speak with a professional about these feelings. This made all the difference in my life...but it would still be six months before he cut off contact with them, and more than a year before I would summon up the courage to seek therapy. And, to tell you the truth, I don't have a convincing reason why it took either of us so long to take action.

....

Since the time that we had essentially cut ties with Gage, we never forgot about him. Sometimes, he was brought up when we needed to vent about how horribly he'd treated us. Other times, we wondered aloud whether we had been too quick to act, and debated with ourselves and each other to validate our actions in hindsight.

One day, though, while mowing the lawn (which gives me far too much free time to think, apparently), I had a startling and disturbing revelation. Gage must have felt very similarly to how *I* felt, during what I now refer to simply as the "Bad Time" in my life. Had he felt that same hopeless darkness? That same assuredness that he was unwanted, unlovable, and useless? That no one would even care if he faded away and disappeared? Had he felt this exact way, which I now fully understood from a first-person point of view? *And we had left him?*

Oh, shit.

We had hemmed and hawed around the idea for months, but on that day, we set about the work of writing a letter to Gage's mom. Contained within the envelope addressed to her was a second letter, addressed to Gage, which we asked her to give to him only if she felt that it would not cause him pain by reopening old wounds.

....

The Choice is Mine: Finding Your Fine

Eventually, after weeks of waiting (and, honestly, giving up any hope for a response), Gage answered us with a letter of his own. He essentially shared that, while he didn't have any remaining ill feelings toward us, he was not currently interested in rekindling the relationship, a fact we totally understood and respectfully accepted.

Sometimes in life, you cannot achieve Fine until you admit your mistakes and apologize for them. Even though sending this letter to Gage was scary, I knew that, during the Bad Time, all I had really needed was for someone to reach out, to ask if I was okay, and to genuinely apologize for hurting me. I also knew that our actions were too little and too late, but we learned a heavy lesson in the interim.

Is there someone in your life who needs your apology, or just your emotional assistance? Are you available and in the proper, self-secure space to reach out and help them? If you are, I encourage you to become vulnerable for them, to help them realize the importance and validity of their existence, and, sometimes, involve a professional third party to help them become healthy again. Don't let someone go, when you can tell that they are not Fine. By sharing your Moratorium, you may well save a life.

A Book to Read or Listen to... *13 Reasons Why* by Jay Asher

Chapter #7:
Loving Me Like I Love You

When I first met Ivan Joseph Hartung, I found myself immediately and irrevocably smitten. I had never before met a human being who embodied the perfect mixture of simultaneous hilarity, sensitivity, confidence, and beauty. I wanted so badly to make him laugh, just so that I could watch him giggle and reveal the dimple on his cheek that complimented his brilliant teeth. My own smile became noticeably brighter when I was around him, too. I was shy and unsure of myself as a college student and newly adult woman, but I watched this gorgeous guy from a safe emotional distance as my warm, fuzzy feelings continued to grow. As teammates, we got along perfectly. During travel season for track and field, we could often be found together, flirting by the hotel pool or getting in trouble for breaking curfew with our friends.

Eventually, during a spring break trip to Arizona, our mutual crush became too obvious for one of our fellow athletes to bear. Sara (a hammer thrower from the country of Serbia) was almost always my roommate when we travelled, and as we arrived back at our room one evening (after an obligatory trip to McDonald's with the rest of the throwers), she asked me, point-blank and with a knowing smile on her face: "Dani, do you like Ivan?"

After taking a moment to slow my racing heart, I answered as coolly as I could. "What? No. Why? What do you mean? Ummm, I mean....Yeah. Oh my gosh, yeah, I do. BUT *DON'T* TELL HIM!" If you have ever been in a similar situation, though, you know two things: 1) Once the cat is out of the bag, you might as well shout from the rooftops that you have feelings for someone, because they are going to find out eventually; and 2) Serbians are not particularly known for their subtlety. Throughout the rest of the trip, Sara made a game of shooting me quick, smirking glances when we were all three together, which made me squirm with some new-to-me combination of delight and mortification. I liked the guy a lot, yes, but I didn't want him to *know*! But there seemed to be tiny sparks beginning to grow for him, too...maybe? In fact, he even (jokingly, I thought) invited me to cuddle at one point during team down time, and I quickly refused because, you know, we weren't married and I was terrified of physical contact.

When we got back to Kansas, the rest of our teammates began to join in Sara's hilarity. Comments were made about us making it "Facebook official, already," and, as Ivan and I spent more and more time together outside of practice, my suspicions about *his* feelings began to grow stronger. On one night in particular, while watching the movie *Ted* as a group, he kinda-sorta put his arm around me, resting it on the top of the couch behind my head...but nothing more! I got back to my apartment and genuinely cried tears of heartache and frustration. Would this guy ever make a move? I hastily texted Sara, as I knew she would be getting a ride from Ivan to morning weight lifting. She agreed to ask him if he liked me or not, so I could be done with the guessing game, and I sank into a collegiate-level slumber.

...When I woke up the next morning, however, I opened my eyes and immediately descended into panic mode. What had I done? How embarrassing was it that I needed a friend to ask a boy out for me, *in college*?? I made a beeline for Sara the instant I got to the weight room. She told me under her breath that she couldn't broach the subject during their ride that morning, because someone else was unexpectedly in the car with them. I sighed audibly. "Oh, thank *goodness*," I said in a hushed tone. "Please, forget about the whole thing. Don't ask him anymore, okay?" She nodded, and we set about our workout.

While eating breakfast with my roommates two hours later, though, I got a surprise call from my persistent friend. "Hi, Dani!" she said excitedly, in a Serbian accent that was quite thick at the time. "I told Ivan that you want to be with him. He loves you, too!" Shocked and thrilled all at once, I collected my jaw from the floor, hung up with my matchmaker, and told my roommates the whole story. (Funnily enough, Ivan and I didn't initially discuss Sara's involvement, though now we credit her greatly for expediting the onset of our relationship.) And, as fate would have it, that week, Ivan began to pay even closer personal attention to me. He would stay after practice to visit, invite me to lunch, and text me on a pretty constant basis whenever we weren't together.

Eventually, I broke my no-cuddle rule, and our favorite pastime became watching movies on the couch at his house. By that point, I had been struggling with severe anxiety about my feelings for this dude -- not because they were fading at all, but because they were *growing* faster than I ever thought possible. I feared that I was taking things too seriously, and that, if he suspected that I was already head-over-heels for him, he might be less inclined to continue in...whatever it was that we were doing. After revealing these fears to him one evening, I felt sure that he would seal his assurances with our first kiss. However, I was more than a little disappointed when he did no such thing.

I drove back to my apartment and immediately laid out the situation for my roommates, hoping for some clarity. I didn't understand why he hadn't kissed me! Like, could I have been any more clear? "You know what?" asked my friend Kendra, a rower from Texas with a hilarious sense of humor and no discernable filter. "This is silly. You need to nut up and go back over there and kiss this man." I nodded slowly, mulling over this notion. And then, I did the only logical thing I could think to do.

I nutted up.

I got back into my car, drove to his house, knocked on the door, and asked his roommate if he was still awake. When he came outside, he asked, wide-eyed, "Am I in trouble?"

"No," I answered, leading him briskly down the front steps to the driveway.

"Are you sure?"

"Ummm...no."

I whirled around to face him before I lost my nerve.

"Listen," I rushed, my heart rattling my ribcage so loudly I was sure he could hear it, "I don't ever do anything like this. Like, never. But I just came back over here because I need to do something, okay?"

And with that, there was no time to lose. I leaned swiftly in toward him, closing my eyes and hoping for a miracle. But, unfortunately, what I actually got was a would-be kissing partner who lit-er-ally *backed away*. All I could think was, *Fuuuuuuuuucccccckkkkkin' cool, bro. My life's over now, bye.* Then, though, I heard the confusion in his voice as he said, "You need to do what?...What are you...**Ohhhh!**" And with that "oh" of realization, he leaned back in to meet me in the middle, where I stood with my eyes literally still closed and my heart in my throat.

And we friggin' kissed!

It was magical and frightening and liberating and exciting and made me feel like a total badass!

I wish I could say that it marked the end of my love-induced anxiety. However, as anyone who knows me will tell you, when asked where my worry actually "ends," I will answer by quoting my favorite movie, *Mean Girls*: "The limit does not exist!" It was a full two months after Ivan "asked me out" before I felt satisfied that he wanted me to be his actual girlfriend. But, despite my nerves, our relationship was going well, and progressed quickly thereafter. Three months in, we were using the "l-word," and after eight months, we moved in together (well, I moved in with him and his roommates). We did everything together, from practice to summer workouts to coaching. It was awesome! We didn't *ever* fight, and we were fairly certain that we never would. We just loved each other too much!

Mmm. Young love.

In typical fashion, real change began to occur between us the year that Ivan graduated from college (I still had one more year to go). Suddenly, he was working while I was in class, and when I was at practice he had free time to make new friends and pick up solo hobbies. In hindsight, this in itself was not at all unhealthy. However, it did come as a great shock to me, as I had grown accustomed to his undivided attention -- and sharing in every experience with him, together as a couple. Now, I was FaceTiming him from my hotel room while travelling for a track meet, as he partied with people I didn't really know, having a smashing time. I felt left out and anxious all over again, worried that he would grow bored of the little routine we had built, preferring instead to spend time with individuals who didn't seem to suffer from social unease at all (unlike me).

As time wore on, we entered into the Bad Time, mentioned in the previous chapter. The more I squeezed and argued and restricted, the more smothered Ivan felt. On the other hand, the more he rebelled and fibbed and retorted, the less valuable I saw myself and the more depressed I became. Eventually, he started to leave me behind when hanging out with friends whose behavior made me increasingly uncomfortable. To avoid more fighting, he would tell me half-truths and sometimes even outright lie about their conversations and whereabouts. And so the cycle continued, with me struggling against the feeling that we were becoming distant, thereby giving him an excuse to continue the charade.

For a time, this conflict grew to be incredibly and constantly toxic. Even though we were engaged by this point, we also *engaged* in serious verbal and emotional fights on a daily basis. Unbeknownst to Ivan, I was sinking further and further into my depression, feeling like I couldn't talk to him about it for fear of appearing manipulative. Even after we moved back to my hometown to buy a house and finish planning our upcoming wedding, the lies, panic attacks, yelling matches, and hurt feelings continued. It wasn't until a few months after our honeymoon that things started to take a turn for the better.

One afternoon, I had had enough. We had been working through the worst of our tension, but Ivan still had not cut ties with the root of our issues. From half a state away, he was still in contact with those friends who excluded, degraded, and ignored me...and he still wasn't being entirely truthful about it. On that particular day, I snapped. After a curt but fiery conversation, he came to the realization, finally, that this behavior was hurting me in a way that could never be erased by any amount of time, so long as it continued. What we needed was action. We needed him to make a choice, if we were going to have a successful marriage. I left things in his hands, and I asked him, for the sake of my own self-worth and the health of our love, to make a final decision.

So, he did.

He made the active (and ongoing) decision to choose me, and to choose *us*. Though it was a long time coming, this choice seemed sudden, after a year and a half of conflict over it. Even today, when I ask him why, or what changed, he will say, "I just realized that you are the most important thing in the world to me. I am sorry I ever hurt you, and I would take it back if I could. You are my person, and I was young and dumb and not thinking of how it made you feel." He had known for some time that this moment would come. He had known all along that, sometimes, it is necessary to make sacrifices for one's partner, when all other avenues have been exhausted. He made the most mature and loving decision I could have asked for, and for that I will be grateful forever.

It has been almost two years since that day, and the aftermath of the Bad Time still affects me in my worst moments. However, we came out of that experience even closer than before, and even more deeply in love than I ever knew we could be. We talk often about how neither of us could fathom going backwards, to a time when we didn't want to spend all of our free time together. After a long day at work, there is no one else I can't wait to talk to, and my "alone time" often includes my husband. From travelling the world to cooking a spaghetti dinner, I cherish each interaction because Ivan is truly my best and most precious friend. However, we check in on each other often, to gauge how each of us are feeling and what each of us needs. It's not that we never fight anymore, but our arguments are constructive and much more sensitive to both of us. We try not to hit below the belt, and we always apologize afterward.

I have learned that it is good for him to play golf with the guys when he misses his friends and the game, and that this doesn't mean that they're not my friends, too, or that he is bored or embarrassed by my presence. I have learned that my husband needs a heavy dose of adventure in his life, and so we do our best to plan accordingly, both socially and financially. On the other hand, he has learned that I need to hear and know how much I mean to him, both in his affirming words and interactions with and around others. And, most importantly, we have both learned to talk about all these things often, so they don't get bottled up until they explode.

I love this man more than anything in the entire world. I feel loved and wanted and valued by him, and I laugh until my belly hurts every single day! We aren't perfect people (no one is), but we have worked together to build such a perfect love out of a "Bad" place, that it makes me tear up just thinking about it. We have been through the fire and made it out on the other side, when it would have been easy to give up. We grew and matured together, making *us* our number-one priority, over anything or anyone else.

Through all this, though, the most important lesson I learned from the Bad Time wasn't that I needed to love Ivan more. Actually, it was that I needed to love *myself* first.

You see, in my little head, somewhere along the line, I created this ideal image of what romantic love would look like -- and, in fact, this perspective has spilled over into my familial and platonic relationships as well. According to my thought process, in order to love, I necessarily had to *sacrifice*. I needed to pour forth from my proverbial "cup" every last bit of energy and affection and attention that I could possibly muster, and then some. And then, at the end of the day, when my cup was bone dry and I could hardly carry on, I expected someone to do the same for me. I expected Ivan to give me a thousand percent of himself, all the time, because I made the mistaken assumption that, if only I emptied myself wildly and constantly, someone would have to fill me back up. That's how love works, right? Aren't those the *rules*?

Oh, how much we learn through trial and error! Poor little twenty-three-year-old Dani's intentions were certainly coming from a good place; her execution, however, was sloppy and counterintuitive. What I should have been doing, rather than spraying my love and energy all over the damn place like a well-shaken two-liter bottle with the lid off, was to give of myself *purposefully*, taking care to maintain a hefty minimum level of self-love in my cup at all times. What I have learned is that, even though my erroneous methods may have *looked* like love, they were actually a mere cry for extrinsic acceptance. What I know now is that I cannot give what I do not have -- and, further, I cannot share with others what I do not feel within and for myself. If I deplete all stores of love within my own heart, then I have nothing to offer to my friends, family, co-workers, or husband. And even if they do wish to share some of their own energies with me, I cannot be so selfish as to presume that they should give it *all* away. After all, they need to stay "full" as well!

The Choice is Mine: Finding Your Fine

Although love does contain within it the caveat that both parties are *willing* to sacrifice for the other, it does not require daily martyrdom or emotional self-mutilation. In fact, these feelings are the opposite of what love is and should be. If you were or are like me, you may have a difficult time fathoming self-love as necessary to genuine devotion to someone else. I, however, would argue urgently that it *absolutely* is. Even if you need help from your partner or friend to pick yourself up when you feel down, you *must* reserve some love, grace, and tenderness for yourself. Otherwise, resentment will grow when neither party feels fulfilled. You want to love them? Then love *you*, friend.

On days when you find it difficult to love yourself the *most*, at least try to love yourself *first*. Don't pour out every drop in your cup -- those around you might be too busy with their own shit to notice it (consider, perhaps, that you gave in an un-empathetic way), and they also might not realize that you are in desperate need of a refill. The person who knows you best is the one who is in charge of what and when you share, giving of yourself *purposefully* by loving you and maintaining some sweetness in that beautiful cup of yours. The next time you're feeling emotionally "empty," give this seemingly backwards thought process a try. It takes practice, sure, but your loved ones will be better off for your self-centered Moratorium.

....

As my husband falls asleep first (like he does every night), following a long and exhausting day at work, I stare at this snoozing beauty for a long and stolen moment. After different towns, houses, jobs, years, and seasons, I still get butterflies when I indulge in a stolen moment to really, truly look at him. I tuck myself in, flick off the light, and kiss my best friend good-night. I send a reply text and set a reminder for tomorrow morning's coffee date. I sigh as I drift off to sleep, mentally affirming my self-love and letting go of the day's stresses. I am content -- first, because I love me; second, because I get to share that love with this amazing hunk snoring softly beside me.

A Book to Read or Listen to... *Big Magic* by Elizabeth Gilbert.

Chapter #8:
Treat Yourself to a Lip Gloss

The fallen leaves surround the back porch at my babysitter's house. I lick the edible Lip Smackers off my lips and do my best rendition of the Backstreet Boys' "Bye, Bye, Bye" choreography. My friends and I are putting on a concert for the other kids, and we are absolutely killing it.

When we go back inside for a snack, I see all the games, toys, and movies that my friends have, and my pop star persona melts swiftly into jealousy and discontent. Wouldn't I be happier if I had all of this stuff? Why can't I buy the new Britney Spears CD?

You may hate me, I thought silently, but it ain't no lie. I wanna cry, cry, cryyyy!

....

....

When I was a younger gal, I would (like many other girls and women in my life) relieve the occasional stressor by dropping a shitload of money on stupid crap I didn't need. Didn't do so well on a test? *Buy a new slap bracelet.* Sad because your crush rejected you? *I know just what you need -- a new, fuzzy blanket, a DVD copy of* The Princess Diaries, *and a Mountain Dew slushie.* Rough week at work? *I think it's about time to buy a new car!*

I have to admit that, while these purchases never fixed the problems I was experiencing, they did solidify the "treat yo self" philosophy I was experimenting with, because I felt the direct effects of valuing myself enough to spend money on something I wanted. This, in turn, made me feel like I must truly love myself! (I mean, you wouldn't ever spend money on someone you didn't really love...would you?) Of course, a neuroscientist would probably say that, by purchasing material objects for myself, I was simply releasing dopamine somewhere in my body, but that all sounds kind of technical and gross, and that's never been my strong suit. I was in this self-love relationship for the *feels*.

A grave misconception of some self-aware, earthy feminists, I think, is that, in order to remain genuine and refrain from appearing materialistic, all of our self-care rituals must come in the form of yoga classes, camping trips, and moderately neglected armpit hair. All of these things are *great*, don't get me wrong! However, I would like to submit that it is possible that the most honest expression of oneself may include the occasional frivolous shopping spree. We, being the evolved and aware adults that we are, realize that this is a band-aid fix, but the band-aid sure looks purty! You say "Sun Salutation"; I say, "instant gratification". You feel me?

My mom attempted to protect me from a lifetime of disappointment and overdraft fees by encouraging me to give in to the retail therapy urge -- in *small*, immediate ways. "It's really true that buying something for yourself can make you feel better," she would say, "but you can achieve that without buying something big. Buy yourself a new nail polish or lip gloss, and there you go! You have treated yourself without spending a lot of money." I absolutely *loved* this philosophy and ran with it for about the next fifteen years.

If I wanted a new outfit but money was tight, I would scour clearance racks and Goodwill hangers for an adorable new dress (that had *pockets* and only cost me $4!). If I felt like I needed a good, old-fashioned spa night, I would buy a face mask sample packet and some 99-cent bubble bath -- and feel like an absolute queen! The great thing about this perspective was that I could buy *more* things, *more* often...because I was spending less on myself each time. It was truly a bliss characterized by quantity over quality, and in my mind, I was living the dream.

The long-term outcome of this lifestyle, though, was twofold -- and only one of the folds was relatively positive. First, the positive: as a result of my love of the lip-gloss-therapy method, I perfected the valuable skill of thriftiness. I wore my keen eye for slashed prices like a badge of honor and worked tirelessly to convert others to the practice I had committed myself to: The Order of the Bargain Shopper.

I discovered online promotional codes and vowed that I would never again buy anything without at least a Google search for "Free Shipping with Purchase Over $25" or some other discount that companies were practically *begging* me to save money with. Craigslist became my favorite social media platform, and I revelled in the used-price ("but in perfect condition!") furniture I could afford to adorn my home with. The only limits to my spending power laid within my own motivation to search high and low for the best deal.

Unfortunately, as you may have guessed, this also meant that I promptly filled my house with a whole heaping lot of *shit*. Trinkets and throw pillows and workout equipment quickly filled up the rooms of the house I shared with my then-fiance. It wasn't until we moved out, exclaiming once every fifteen minutes, "When did we get all this stuff? How can this much crap fit inside a house??" that we realized that we (*ahem*...I) might have a thrift-induced problem.

I had allowed my feigned self-love to overtake the physical space I lived in. I mean, after all, I was truly only attempting to buy my own affections. By substituting purchases for self-respect, I was treating myself like the stepson who hates my guts and refuses to look me in the eye. I had mistaken that damn dopamine for an actual, genuine love for me -- and, rather than buying myself the occasional treat *because* of this love, I was buying useless shit *instead* of building a healthy, confident self-concept. And I had practically become a professional at doing this on a constant basis, since I had discovered that I could fool myself on a budget. Hence, the negative fold.

I am not a hoarder, by any means, and particularly after watching a Netflix documentary on minimalism, Ivan and I have truly (and quite literally) cleaned up our act. We stop and think before we buy physical objects for our home, and when we do splurge we prefer it to be on experiences and quality time spent with friends. We sell and donate extra stuff often, and we recognize the importance of preventing our space from becoming too "noisy". But now that I have stopped utilizing my clearance rack parlor tricks as a means to validate my worth, I have been forced to search for other ways to fill the void. Like, for example, actually liking myself in lasting and substantial ways.

For the record, none of this is to debunk the real, albeit short-term, effectiveness of good, old-fashioned retail therapy (utilized sparingly). I also love-love-love the thrill I get from finding the best possible price on something I have legitimate use for, and I still buy the occasional lip gloss on an off-kilter day. However, I am now newly and fiercely committed to practicing more holistic rituals of self-love. To do this, I got right back to my hippie roots and adopted the following "I Heart Dani" habits:

Dani's Favorite Happy Habits (in no particular order):

1. Dress how I feel

Some days, I want to dress like a boss, in power pants and pointed dress shoes. Other days (most days), I feel more like myself when I am in yoga pants and a racerback tank -- rocked in conjunction with the ever-blessed sports bra. This look makes me feel both comfy and ready for athletic action at a moment's notice. It makes me feel unrestricted and youthful, and *owning* athletic clothes motivates me to *use* them by exercising regularly.

2. Watch my posture

I have always, always slumped forward in my shoulders. They are large-and-in-charge forces, but they tend to look insecure because they roll forward and cause me to slouch. An adolescence of unchecked, rehab-less weightlifting and shot put throwing did not help my unbalanced upper body muscle structure. I utilize yoga and regular stretching in order to combat this issue, but I have also found that keeping mindful of my posture, and changing it purposefully when I notice the slump, does wonders for my self-confidence. Power stance to the rescue!

3. Drink more water

Oh, trust me. I know that this one is hard. But there isn't much to say here, except that it's good for us and we all need to do a better job of it. Drink up!

4. Up the veggies

Just like a clever mommy who is raising the infant of her own eating habits, I find it oddly satisfying to "trick" my mind into thinking I'm eating carb-y foods, when I'm actually (shhhh!) eating *vegetables*! Pinterest is chock-full of veggie substitutions, like butternut squash spaghetti noodles or carrots cut in the shape of crinkly potato chips. And, while your brain isn't stupid -- it can obviously tell the difference between carrot and spud -- the *crunch!* feeling is still just as satisfying, making it a wonderful substitute for the willing and open mind.

5. Focus on those brows

If you could only use one, single makeup product for the whole day, what would you choose? For me, it would likely be my eyebrow goop! In middle school, as soon as I discovered the mighty power of tweezers, I quickly let their power lead me astray. I plucked the absolute snot out of my brows until there was but a pencil-thin line remaining. Tragic (but also, at the time, trendy).

Since then, I have tried and then sworn off waxing, finally making the commitment to growing out my eyebrows to a satisfactory length and level of bushy-ness. I maintain them myself, and their improvement has dramatically changed my first-glance appearance.

Whether you'd choose mascara, lipstick, or nothing at all, it's okay to be proud of (and play up) your best features, to a level that makes *you* feel happy!

The Choice is Mine: Finding Your Fine

Remember to maintain the delicate balance between treating yourself because you deserve it...and using unnecessary purchases to create a false sense of self-love. Buy things that will make you happy over the long term, not just for today! And if you do need that one-time pick-me-up, I would suggest that you search for purchases that don't take up space in your home: for example, a bath bomb that will dissolve or a happy-hour margarita that will disappear right down the hatch.

It takes mindfulness and self-love to identify when it is best to utilize retail therapy -- and when you need to pump the breaks. Know that it is fine to treat yourself from a place of genuine love and self-care, being cognizant of the fact that you cannot buy your own affections...only dopamine.

A Book to Read or Listen to... *Big Magic* by Elizabeth Gilbert

Chapter #9:
Trust in Your Tomorrow Self

I am meditating, in a seated position with my hands on my tummy. I am focusing on the in-and-out motion of my breath, clearing my mind of the day's frustrations. My intention for this meditation?

Fuck It.

I have text messages to answer, laundry to wash, carpet to vacuum, dinner to make, and writing to do...but right now, in this moment, I need the strength to say, "Fuck all that for the time being. I am here, and I am focused on this."

I have to reach down deep into my heart and remind myself that I will be just as capable of completing those tasks ten minutes from now as I am in this moment. Nothing will break, no one will die, and the world will not come to an end, if I just take this time and focus it solely on myself, right now.

....
....

As a person with naturally high self-motivation and an admitted teacher's pet complex, I can sometimes have a teeeeeensy bit of a difficult time delegating the worries of the world to anyone else. For example, I often find myself sighing loudly at my laundry list of monthly tasks, *tsk-tsk*-ing in alarm at the prospect of not being able to accomplish them all *today*. Keep in mind, I am referring to my "To-Do" list for an entire month-long span. And yet, somehow, I can manage to stress myself out about the fact that these duties are not *already completed*. Why do I do this to myself??

Well, part of me is probably a little bit of a martyr. I desire the reputation of a hard-working Wonder Woman, someone who can accomplish every task in record time without either collapsing or complaining. I want others to view me as "dependable," and so, like a creepy clown shaping an oblong balloon into a squeaky animal-ish figure, I have warped the concept of dependability into synonymy with self-sacrifice. *Noticing a recurring theme here, eh?*

Somewhere along the line, you see, I picked up the idea that in order to love someone, I had to empty myself of all my energy and self-love *for* them. In order to show someone love, respect, or dependability, I felt that I had to work myself to the bone and *sacrifice*, whether or not sacrifice was necessary. I constantly emptied my cup at the feet of every person I interacted with. This became most problematic when, expecting a refill of the other person's every ounce of energy in return...I consistently came up short. This would result in crushing self-hatred due to the belief that, if others did not do for me emotionally as I felt obligated to do for them, that they must, most definitely, hate me.

This tendency, which I am working to correct both in my psyche and habitual existence, can sometimes spill over into my work-life balance, especially during times of high stress. It makes me feel both relieved and competent when I overwork myself, because this is the easiest metric to display for others to see.

My aforementioned counselor, Gina, and I had a rousing breakthrough conversation about this other-centric, affirmative need of mine. We spoke about how my background in sports and academics has given me an easy-way-out method for defining my self-worth. In order to feel good about myself, I have developed a need for people to give me a "ranking" or a "grade". It is so much easier to know where I stand if there is an objective metric associated with my actions. And, in the absence of any of these, I would much prefer to have people "cheering in the stands" (as at track meet), verbally approving of my work.

"Do you see?" I metaphorically shout at them. "Don't you see what I've done? I've given up everything else -- blocked out *everything* else -- in order to complete these tasks. And behold! I have crossed *every one of them* off my list! No one can claim that I'm lazy or uncaring -- the proof is in my toil and under-eye circles!"

Now, this tactic (though still highly unhealthy) worked quite well when I was an undergraduate bachelorette, owing my time to no one but myself and choosing to spend it, far more often than not, on *accomplishing* than on silly ventures like empathizing or relationship building. However, I now lead a beautiful life, which includes far more fulfilling endeavors than crossing errands off of a list.

Aside from my cuddly pets and wanderlusting heart, I have a hilarious and gorgeous husband who cares little about the opinions of others but who needs a healthy dose of FUN each day in order to keep his energy frequency high. He isn't wired to put on blinders and work himself into oblivion like me; this doesn't bring him personal satisfaction. He is a more relational and adventuresome being, which I admire and fall more deeply in love with every moment. This does, however, require a measure of wholehearted attention each day from his wife, causing quite the mental wrestling match between my devotion to him and my deeply ingrained need to perform this habit of constant self-sacrifice.

He needs my love and laughter, but if I stop to joke and relax...how will I prove that I am devoted to him? To my work? To crossing shit off my checklist?? ...Are you starting to see how backward this all sounds?

Another factor that adds to this conundrum is that I have told myself for many years that, "If you just *do the task now*, then you'll have more time for Ivan and the rest of your life *later*. This way, it's off your mind, you know? You can check it off, and *then* go back to giggling over an episode of *Brooklyn Nine-Nine*."

So, what is my solution to this well-intentioned chaos? I present to you the idea of my "Tomorrow Self." This concept simply implies that, in space and time, there is only one *current me* -- only one Right Now Self. The "Dani" I will be an hour or a week or ten years from now is a completely different human, who can be treated with the reverence and trust of a dear friend (because, well, she *is*). I can trust in my Tomorrow Self to complete tasks that *she* receives, in her own time and place...rather than trying to accomplish them all *for* her, in the present moment. Right Now Dani needs to stay in her lane!

The Choice is Mine: Finding Your Fine

The beauty of the Tomorrow Self, among other things, is that Ivan is married to *both* of us. But, though he loves us both, he would prefer that I give my chores and worries to my Tomorrow Self while we are together, so that he can hang out with *me, right now.*

Recently, my co-worker brought his one-year-old son to our office for a visit. This experience offered me an eye-opening perspective on my own constant wish for others' approval. Baby's parents were teaching him the basic principles of throwing, and they would encourage him by cheering, "Yayyy! Good job!" after every satisfactory toss of a toy. During the cheers, the little guy would join in by clapping for himself and grinning widely, obviously pleased by the attention and validation he received from the adults in the room.

After a few rounds of this, all the grown-ups began to chat, looking temporarily away from the tot, who they assumed was finished throwing. While no one else was looking, his little chubby toddler hands heaved the toy yet again, and he looked expectantly around the room, readying himself for a round of "*Hooray*!s" and literally holding his chubby little arms up, poised in a clap-ready position. But...no one had seen him throw it. Wade's face fell as his eyes glanced from person to person, and then he began to look confused (and even *concerned*) that no one was cheering for him.

As I watched this tiny person teeter on the edge of an imminent breakdown, I realized that, in much the same way, I have been acting like a baby. I have made it the rest of the world's responsibility to affirm me, even for things that cannot be fairly measured or observed, like, for example, how hard I work at my job or how great of a wife and friend I am.

In the end, it's more important to be fine with who you are right now, regardless of how others react to your actions. This is why we practice daily affirmations! You have to find your sense of Fine on an introspective level, because the world will not clap and cheer for you (at least not for very long) when you hit your recruitment numbers, answer a text message, or cook a wicked chicken marsala. Chasing this type of false confidence is a waste of your energy and the life of your Right Now Self. But YOU can change the grading scale!

It's an insult to yourself not to trust the Tomorrow version of you with your to-do list -- she is capable. Hand it over! Instead of saying, "Oh, my gosh! I'm so stressed that I can't do all of these tasks right this second!" switch to, "You know what? My Tomorrow Self is awesome, and I'm going to entrust this to her. She is going to knock it out of the park in the morning." Shoot, you may even need to bypass the Tomorrow Self and give some shit to your Someday Self, a distant, vague cousin who holds onto dreams and ambitions we don't have the brain space for just yet.

View life as an effort grade, for you *and* others. It's not pass/fail, but a feeling. How do you feel about *you* today? That's where you need to start. And from there, head toward Fine.

A Book to Read or Listen to... *Junie B. Jones Is a Beauty Shop Guy* by Barbara Parks

Chapter #10:

Unpacking's No Small Thing

It is the spring of 2012. I startle at the sound of my 5:30 am phone alarm and rub my eyes gingerly open as I hit the touchscreen "STOP" button. I think, grumpily, about how wish there was a "fuck this" button. I toss my single throw blanket to the side and climb down from my bed, which is lofted and, underneath my formerly sleeping body...<u>*fully made.*</u>

I also slept in my track and field gear, so there is no need to change. I slip off the surface of my comforter and into some Nike tennis shoes and then grab my backpack as I stumble out into the darkened hallway of my dorm. I don't have any time to dawdle if I am going to walk to the parking lot, locate my car, and drive to team weightlifting by 6:00 am.

....

Collegiate track and field was an incredibly formative experience for me. I flew on a plane for the first time and visited several states I never would have even dreamed about in my youth. I gained massively improved time management skills, and I made friends from all over the world. There is one thing, though, that this privilege did not help me to develop. In all my years as an athlete, a college student, a young adult...I never learned how to *take up space*!

This embarrassing unwillingness to proudly occupy the physical area around me manifested itself in awkward (*eccentric,* I would tell myself) and unorthodox ways. For example, I would never un-make my bed in order to go to sleep, because I didn't want to ever get comfortable enough that I might oversleep my alarm for morning weights. When I would travel with the team, even when we stayed in a place for several days, I would never fully unpack my suitcase, keeping my things perfectly organized and tucked neatly away so as to control my possessions and prevent myself from leaving anything behind when we left.

I was in a constant state of discomfort and unease. It was as though the Universe was whispering, "Hon, it's okay...take off your coat and stay awhile," and I couldn't hear her because I was too busy nervously humming to myself and picking out tomorrow's clothes so that I could wear them as tonight's PJs. What I didn't realize at that time was that this display of rigid "self-shrinkage" was truly a projection of my insecure emotional state.

As a small-town girl from western Kansas, I always wanted to attend college -- but it wasn't until high school that I began to dream about the possibility of being a prospective NCAA Division-I college athlete. I fell in love with my school and team the first time I visited, and the rest was, as they say, history. However, life in the "big city" (truly, it was just a bigger small town, but I didn't know it yet), was not exactly like I thought it would be.

I was constantly getting lost and feeling quite small in my giant, overflowing lecture classes. My dorm floor-mates didn't initially understand how a town the size of Plainville *existed* in 2011, let alone had *indoor plumbing*. Even some of my more elitist teammates considered me "just a thrower," as if my steadily climbing weight and lack of assigned cardio work equated directly to a loss of athleticism and dedication. Much of the experience of the first several months of college made me wish desperately for Harry Potter's invisibility cloak...I was, by no stretch of the imagination, confident in my new space, or my right to be there.

For the first time in my life, I began to experience frequent and debilitating panic attacks, in which my chest would rapidly tighten into hyperventilation, after which I would cry uncontrollably (fortunately for me, my roommate was an active member of the school's marching band, and very rarely home). These episodes would follow me for the next several years and, over the course of that time, cause me to miss shifts at part-time jobs and (more than once) call on a track coach to graciously rescue me from the demons in my own mind. I am forever grateful for the people in my life who helped me through these attacks, without judgement or irritation.

However, their patience and love didn't stop, or even lessen, the anxiety. And this chronically panicked existence I was now living eventually began to gnaw away at my internal sense of worth. Slowly but surely, the theme of my life became: "You don't deserve _____, because you are literally such a hot mess." I didn't feel that I deserved friendship, so I pushed my peers and teammates away, often declining invitations and throwing myself into my schoolwork as a foolproof excuse. I didn't think that I deserved the affections of my then-boyfriend, Ivan, so I became paranoidly convinced that it was only a matter of time before I became "too much" for him and worried constantly that it would cause him to break up with me at any moment.

I was becoming, for all intents and purposes, an emotional hermit. I wanted desperately to join my teammates, classmates, and friends who frolicked effortlessly through a "normal college experience." I, on the other hand, was fighting an invisible battle in my head, every day. Remember, this was before my anxiety brought along our dear third wheel, depression. This was pure, unprecedented and unsolicited, high-functioning anxiety. I didn't want to live like this, but I truly didn't know how (or what) to change.

Fast-forward to today, through a myriad of heart-to-hearts, attempts at medication, and months of therapy, and you might note the differences in my behavior:

It is 2018. I have just driven myself to the hotel in my university recruiting territory. I confidently tell the front-desk manager my name and compliment her glimmering manicure. I make my way up to the room, where I FaceTime my husband to let him know that I arrived safely, and then I immediately set to work unpacking my shit all over the place.

In the bathroom, I unload my hair products, make-up, and shower items and arrange them neatly on the counter, much like they would be placed at my house. I choose the queen bed closest to the door (always) and spread my fuzzy personal blanket over the top of the bedspread, just after fluffing the sheets to untuck them from the foot of the mattress. Next, I utilize the other queen as my "stuff bed," where I sprawl out the remaining contents of my suitcase and computer bag.

I set about cooking myself a dinner of soup and French bread, and then flop down on the armchair to relax in my temporary "home."

....

....

What caused this shift in my outlook and ability to confidently take up space? Honestly, this one is as simple as the old adage, "Fake it 'til you make it"! The honest-to-goodness truth is this: When I made the decision to stop allowing myself to emotionally shrink -- to act as though I am worthy of the space I can't help but take up -- I wasn't *all that* sure about it.

Sometimes, I have found, it is necessary for me to put action before belief, in order to replace my old, destructive self-fulfilling prophecies with new, affirming ones. Before, I would think things like, *No one* truly *wants to be my friend, so I should decline this party invitation and stay home.* Funny how things work -- I ended up with fewer and fewer social invitations, when, in fact, I can see now that the original offers were genuine and sent from a place of love.

Today, on the other hand, I will tell myself things like, *My friends love me and want to spend time with me. I should text them and see if they are free to hang out!* Even though there is sometimes still a rude little narrator in my mind, telling me that they will roll their eyes and say, "*Gross...Dani again?*", I go through my daily affirmations, kick myself in the pants, and text them, telling myself all the while that, "They love me. They love me. They love me."

In this way, I practice taking up emotional space, just like I proudly occupy the physical space of my hotel room. I tell myself that I am 1) worthy; 2) deserving; and 3) loved, over and over again. And you know what? I am starting to believe it! And this belief serves as the catalyst for a snowball effect of self-esteem, -love, and -affirmation (rinse, and repeat). Being stubborn enough to forcibly take up both actual and psychological space (as opposed to making myself lonely and emotionally unavailable in order to avoid pain that likely never would have occurred), allows me the confidence to continue the cycle.

The Choice is Mine: Finding Your Fine

Do you struggle to feel worthy of people's time? Affection? Respect? Love? Two things:

1. I am here to tell you that YOU ARE WORTHY.
2. I am also here to tell you that MY WORDS ARE NOT ENOUGH.

There is nothing I can do or say to convince you that you are worthy. Your psyche wants to hear from *you*, friend! Your heart needs to hear you whisper the vulnerable affirmations you have set out to solidify, in order to strengthen the proper synapses in your brain and make self-love your HABIT.

Did you know that, some days, Adrienne Michaels doesn't feel like going to the gym? I don't know her personally (yet), but I would be willing to bet that even this great, super fit, amazingly motivational beast of a human being has certain days when she is just tired and bummed and stressed and doesn't want to get out of bed or eat healthy foods. But guess the hell what? Adrienne has built muscles and created habits that can both push her through a slump and allow her some "wiggle room" to miss the occasional workout or eat a brownie every now and again.

In the exact same way, you need to work out your self-love muscles. You need to search for "fine" every day through verbal (out *loud*!) affirmations and small, significant acts of taking up just the right amount of space -- which, spoiler alert, is just the *exact* amount of space you *deserve* to take up! Shout "I LIVE HERE RIGHT NOW!" to the Universe, wherever you go. You have to establish in your own mind where you live, so that you can really and truly *live*. Spread out, make a mess, fart freely, and claim a territory that is yours and yours to share.

Make Moratorium your daily mental space, in which you give yourself loving, gracious permission to have a bad day, but not to let that allow a negative spiral of self-hatred to manifest in your life. Love yourself in the ways you *treat* yourself, regardless of whether you initially buy into your own worthiness...you might be surprised in the newfound philosophies you start to pick up along the way.

A Book to Read or Listen to... *The City of Ember* by Jeanne DuPrau

Chapter #11:
Your Friends Have Dirty Bathrooms, Too

Swiftly, I bustle around my home, straightening a throw pillow here and dusting a shelf there. The sweet aroma of chocolate chip cookies fills the air, and ragtime music plays from my bluetooth speaker. I slip on my patent pumps and straighten my frilly, plaid apron.

I shoo the dogs out into the backyard as I curtly ask my husband to put on some underwear. "What's the big deal?" he asks. "Are we prepping to sell the house or something?"

NOPE!

I'm doing all this because the mailman might come and deliver a package today, and I don't want him to think we live like heathens -- do you? Hmm??

pause for dramatic effect

All this stress and effort for such a little payoff? But...why?

....

Last week, sitting in a booth and talking too loudly while a little tipsy on one-dollar Applebee's drinks, I had an extremely important revelation. I talked around and around the topic with my ever-patient husband, while our waiter swept the shine clean off the floor near our table, passive aggressively letting us know that our very small tab was already paid and we needed to please leave.

The essence of my revelation was this: *If I spend my emotional energy judging others exclusively on their ability and willingness to "save" me, I will inevitably manifest a friendless and frustrating experience of this world.*

This sounds particularly meaty, but bear with me for a moment.

I have, for as far back as I can recall, viewed most of my relationships in terms of what people could do for *me*. I don't mean this as a you-scratch-my-back-I'll-scratch-yours metaphor, mind you. In this scenario, I'm talking more exclusively about a little thing called *emotional capital*. Though I do genuinely love people, it is incredibly easy for me to cut them off if they offend or hurt me in any way. I am learning, however, that this is an unnecessary and inefficient self-defense tactic that has made me appear standoffish and emotionally unavailable.

While I intuitively know that this habit stems, first and foremost, from insecurity, I am in the process of updating my daily habits in order to add a helpful ingredient to my relational life: grace. In the same way that I have stressed my*self* out in the attempt to be perfect, I have applied the same impossible standards to those around me, in some sort of "fair's fair" twisted attempt to make myself feel better for constantly failing to meet these ridiculous expectations.

When I was living in my first college apartment, I would clean every square inch of its common spaces before going home for any "extended" breaks (including the singular, two-day weekend). I would furiously scrub the kitchen counter while glancing at the clock, cursing my roommates for their lack of neuroses and thanking the heavens for the invention of Clorox wipes. If any unexpected holiday guests were to arrive in my absence, or if some home and garden magazine stopped by to photograph our living room for their "World's Okayest Apartment" snapshot series, I wanted it to be *perfect*.

On the other hand, I have always relished the feeling of coming home to a clean house. It's like a little surprise when you arrive back after a long trip -- in the interim, you've almost forgotten about making your bed, and it's as if someone *else* did it while you were away! More to the point, though, I felt as though I couldn't fully relax back home at my parents' house knowing that I hadn't put 100% effort and pride into the presentation of my own living space. Perhaps it was simply environmental control...but, just maybe, there was a darker perspectival assumption at work here.

I have worked hard lately to peel back the layers and unpack this apparently unimportant obsession (which I have continued to this day). Why is it that I feel the need to leave my home spotless for the benefit of others, most especially while I won't even be there? And why (here's the kicker) do I feel *guilty* and *anxious* if I simply don't do it?

The answer came in two parts, most notably in regards to my own behavior. First, though I don't consider myself a materialistic person, I do believe in taking good and loving care of the physical "stuff" that I am blessed with. Second...

I am a liar.

I want my home to appear clean and tidy to visitors, as if that is the way we live all the time (which we definitely don't). But why lie? The answer to this question was the hardest pill to swallow. In essence, I want people to pat me on the butt like the good little girl that I am, because, hello? *I cleaned my whole room by myself!* This way, they'll be so distracted by my efforts that they might not notice the not-so-squeaky-clean skeletons in my closet.

I want my home to look spotless and inviting, because I, myself, am not. I somehow cooked up the subconscious notion that I could cover up my awkward difficulties with emotional attachment by controlling the appearance of the space around me and making it aesthetically pleasing to visitors. Of course, this only works long-term if you can drop the act, foster connections, and convince people to come *back*!

Over the past several years, in which I have purposefully and tirelessly worked to become what I consider to be an all-around "better friend," I have come to the conclusion that, while it is not wrong to respect your things and space, it is wrong to put things and space *before* people and experiences.

It has always been difficult for me to be spontaneous. In fact, I remarked to Ivan just yesterday about the grimly interesting paradox that, for me, it is *harder* work to be "fun" than it is to complete tasks. I have an extremely difficult time with last-minute plans and unexpected changes; they can put me into a state of anxious agitation almost immediately. But as I look at the above analysis of my mental musings, I am forced to reckon with the truth that life is not a prepared or scripted speech. I will not always have the answers, or the words in the right order, or my toilet freshly cleaned. And people might see me for the mess that I am. And I have to be fine with that.

But...HOW?

The Choice is Mine: Finding Your Fine

I have to find Fine in a messy kitchen. In a yard full of leaves. In an unmade bed, in full view from the hallway.

I have to remember that I love my friends, and they love me. I have to remind myself that I don't expect them to have a spotless house, because that would mean they were spending more time cleaning than they were hanging with me and others, creating awesome memories and laughing so hard that soda shoots out their pie holes, right onto the un-vacuumed carpet.

I have to remember that I am worth more than the cleanliness of my space. Although my decor is an expression of my style, a food-covered stovetop does not tell the story of a sloppy housekeeper; rather, it is evidence of the delicious late night quesadillas that were consumed the night before. A messy house isn't "bad" -- it's *just* messy! And it doesn't mean my guests won't enjoy themselves; it just means that I dropped everything to welcome them in.

Overall, this new resolution can be described as: trying not to hide behind tidiness in an effort to conceal the Hot Mess Express that lies within. In terms of day-to-day interactions, it looks like: 1) not gritching at my husband for forgetting to put the hand towel on the hook (where it *clearly* belongs, but I digress); 2) leaving the laundry in the dryer for an extra day, if it means getting to walk the dogs before sunset; 3) not ever, ever, ever again apologizing for the dirty dishes in the sink. My visitor may not have brought their kitchen sink with them to my house...but I know, with certainty, that it is not as empty as I have previously tricked myself into believing.

But I love them, just the same.

Chapter #12:
Show Me The Money!

I am sitting in the passenger seat of James Corden's car. He asks me witty questions about chia seeds and the publication of my first book, and we belly laugh through the streets of New York City while periodically singing songs by Pan!c At The Disco and The Cheetah Girls...just before unveiling my new original song (released earlier that month).

As the final chords fade out, James wipes a happy tear from his eye and peers over at me. "Do you know what I would really love? I would love it if we could sing a song from a movie that I know is close to your heart." Without another word of explanation, James pushes a button on the stereo, and the song From Now On from The Greatest Showman begins to play. My hands are shaking, because this is the moment I've been waiting for. I clear my throat, even through the lump that is beginning to form within it. I sing the first lines through subsequent waves of emotion, and try to keep my breath steady.

Suddenly, sitting up from his concealed place beneath a blanket in the backseat, Hugh Jackman emerges and begins to sing in unison with me. (By this point, I am absolutely bawling, but I somehow still look hot from all the shit the makeup artists put on my face earlier that afternoon.) We hold hands and make totally comfortable eye contact, singing through the lyrics "...but when I STOP and see you here, I remember who all this was foooooooorrr!"

In sync with the word "stop," the car pulls over to the curb, directly in front of Rockefeller Center. I do not have to ask what we are doing here -- I *race to unbuckle my seatbelt and follow Hugh out into the flash mob that is*

already forming. This gigantic group of people is composed of talented,

dancing extras, members of the cast from The Greatest Showman *(including*

both Zac Efron and Zendaya), and my husband, Ivan, followed swiftly by

James, Hugh, and myself.

We sing through the second verse of the song and begin on the chorus,

with crowds of people gathering to watch the increasingly impressive show.

The dancers perform in perfect step behind us, while Hugh and I share a

microphone front and center, belting, "And we will come back hooooooome!

Hoooome agaaaaaiiiiinn!" It takes all that I have not to pee my pants...but I

hold it in.

After the song is finished, I begin to cry again, and I hug Hugh, James,

Zac, and Zendaya, telling them gleefully that I'll never be able to thank them

enough. I run into the arms of my husband (How has he been able to keep this

a secret from me??) and we burst into fits of giddy laughter together.

The scene fades out, and James begins this evening's episode of The Late

Show.

This, friends, is my Very Specific Dream.

....

Every person I have told about this dream has laughed kindly and

undoubtedly assumed that I was joking. I assure you, I am not. This dream is

not a gag to me...I really, desperately, want it to come true, just as I have

described it. When I need a brain break throughout the day, I spend time

fleshing out this musical fantasy, and every time Brendon Urie sings "High

Hopes" I am mentally transported directly to James Corden's car, where we lean in and scream-sing the lyrics together, noting the song's impact on our perspective in times of struggle.

In fact, I commonly refer to specific, emotionally charged, recurring daydreams like this one as "Futuries" (like, the opposite of "memories"). Futuries, for me, are soul food. They are the best motivators because I can truly get lost in them...and when I come out on the other side, I'm willing to do what it takes to achieve them, for real.

The hurdle, I think, that many people have a difficult time overcoming in terms of my Very Specific Dream is that, in order for it to come true, I would have to become both rich and famous. To that logic, I say simply: "YEAH, DUDE!" Then,after any initial bristling at the thought of *desiring* notoriety and fortune, I would love to explain to the naysayers what, exactly, I mean.

What I mean is, *I WANNA BE RICH.*

I want to buy my dream home in Flagstaff, Arizona, on a private plot of land with a killer view of the mountains...and I want to be so debt-free and well-off that I can *plop!* my down payment onto the loan officer's desk with satisfaction. *Or*, screw the whole thing and pay outright for my house -- no mortgage required!

I want to have a moderately sized outbuilding called *The Teal Chameleon* on our property that doubles as a yoga studio and coffee shop, where people can study and hang out, before heading into my signature *Bear Your Buddha Belly* yoga class (patent pending, eventually). I want to be able to offer weekly kids' yoga classes for free as a gift to my community, and I want to do all this on a grade school teacher's salary because I have other forms of supplemental income in which I am absolutely *crushing* it (namely, writing both self-help and children's books).

I want to give my husband a state-of-the-art facility to train for his World Long Drive competitions -- one in which he can practice *and* train new, up-and-coming golfers. I want a huge fenced area behind our house, so that my dogs can frolic and play and be within sight of the back door, as I gaze out the window of my kitchen while cooking dinner for our visiting friends. I deeply desire all of these things, and in order to achieve this level of personal happiness, I will need to grind and get creative in order to make quite a bit of *money*.

If this idea of chasing money makes you uncomfortable or disgusted with me, let me be the first to tell you...I used to be right there with you. It wasn't until I listened to the acclaimed author Jen Sincero speak about money (and the logic behind desiring it) in her book *You Are a Badass* that I began to see my discomfort with financial ambition for the poppycock that it was. In her book, Sincero often references what is known as the Law of Attraction. Now, even if this isn't your cup of earl gray, bear with me for a second.

In order to assess what you will need to achieve your dreams, Sincero asserts, you must first outline, very specifically, what things, experiences, and achievements will make you personally and truly happy. Then, you will need to realign your relationship with money to jive with these goals, to make them possible to accomplish. However (and this is a big caveat, here), if you do not *love* money -- if you think it is dirty and evil and undesirable -- then you will not likely be able to manifest the money you need in order to convert your dreams into reality.

For example, to paraphrase Sincero, if you really like a certain friend and want to hang out with her (because she adds value, fun, and calm to your life) then you wouldn't make snide remarks about every other person who hangs out with her, would you? You wouldn't call her "stuck-up" or "pretentious" and tell all your other friends that you didn't need her to be happy...would you? If you did that, then why the hell would she hang out with you anymore?

Get it?

If you want to attract something into your life, you need to treat it with respect and value it for the positive impact it has on your experience and desires. Such is the case with money. In *You Are A Badass*, Sincero encourages her readers to write a letter to money as if it were a person, to practice the improvement of our energy toward the very dollars we want to strive for. So, in the spirit of practicing what I preach and manifesting a bunch of Benjamins, I decided to give it a shot.

Here goes:

Dear Money,

Hello! I wanted to take the time today to thank you for being an amazing tool for change in my life. When I am smarter and more creative with you, I am able to accomplish my goals (like paying off debts), but I want to spend even more time with you, so that I can achieve these smaller dreams even faster and move on to the big ones (like owning my dream home).

I know that I will need to be innovative and steadfast in order to earn and organize you, but I appreciate that, even in times when it seemed like there wasn't quite enough of you to go around, you always stayed close enough to keep me afloat. I see your impact through the generous people around me, and I love witnessing my neighbors and friends as they utilize you for the betterment of others.

I respect and admire the freedom that you allow people to have in their lives, Money. I desire to manifest this experience for myself and my family, so that our cups can be so full that we are secure in sharing you with those around us, without hesitation or pause to consult The Budget. I want to spend time thinking about you, so that I can envision you only in positive, affirming terms.

We have come a long way in our relationship, friend. I intend to meet you where you are, so that we can continue to strengthen our bond. I am already excited and grateful to be seeing a lot more of you in the near future.

Yours Truly,

Dani

In writing to money, I have exercised my ability to manifest that which I love -- and that which will allow me to pursue the things and life experiences that I love.

Now, writing letters, of course, is not the only method for attracting that which you desire into your life. Another practice I have found quite helpful (after having it suggested to me by multiple authors and friends) is the concept of a Vision Board. Take a "board" (which can be taken to mean anything from a small piece of printer paper to an entire wall that you paint into a chalkboard) and fill it up with symbols of your very own Very Specific Dreams.

In our case, Ivan and I bought a rectangular cork board from the local thrift store and printed out pictures of the places we want to live and travel. In addition, we attached a printed text version of our first financial goal, which reads "Debt-Free by 2021!" The last piece of our vision board may be where I lose the less eccentric in the crowd, but it is working wonders for us so far.

Ivan and I both want to be teachers. In our ideal future, I would be an elementary school teacher in the same district in which he teaches middle school P.E. In order to represent a scenario which obviously hasn't yet occurred, I printed off stock photos of teachers in action...with our faces copied onto their bodies. Do we look a little bit like bobblehead dolls? Absolutely. Do I walk by that vision board every single day and receive visual confirmation (*in advance*) that I would be a super cute teacher, next to my super cute husband, who is also a teacher? You bet your bum.

Based on the premise of this very book, you might have guessed that I find social media to be a great personal motivator. Therefore, it will probably not surprise you that I immediately posted a video of our vision board the moment it was hung on the wall, both to encourage others to follow suit and to ask for people to hold me accountable to this new goal-setting tool. With the song *Mouth of the River* by Imagine Dragons playing in the background, I displayed our hard work for the world to see...and, since that time, several people have encouraged me and asked for my advice in creating their own vision boards.

The purpose of my vision board is for me to look at affirming and aspirational images every single day. They say that goals written down are far more likely to be achieved; well, if a picture's worth a thousand words, then my collage-style vision board is going to help me achieve for years to come! I would highly encourage you to create a vision board of your own. Remember, though, that this doesn't have to be something that takes up a ton of space in your home.

Maybe you create a picture menagerie that you then set as the lock screen on your phone. Maybe you make a tiny, credit-card sized version that spells out your monthly budget and reminds you not to overspend each time you open your wallet. Hell, you can literally go '90s and put sticky notes on your bathroom mirror! My cork board is on the hallway wall just outside of my bedroom. I can see it from a seated position on my bed. As long as your vision "board" is placed strategically in an area that you visit each day (preferably multiple times each day), then it is going to help you to retrain your brain to *know* that you can chase your dreams, because you have given yourself permission to peek into the future that you have committed to creating.

The Choice is Mine: Finding Your Fine

Does your Very Specific Dream include making lots of money? Traveling out of the country? Buying a tuxedo? Taking an acting class? Whatever you want to do, see, buy, experience, or become -- you have to start at the start! And your starting point is re-working your relationships with the tools you will need to achieve your dreams (like money, for example) and affirming your ability to accomplish your goals every day (with some version of the vision board).

I would also like to take the opportunity here to stress that (as mentioned in previous chapters), the quickest way to true happiness is not *stuff*. What honestly, truly, wholly makes you happy? Ask this question *first*, and then set about filling your "now" with pieces, one by one, of the future you desire. And don't take the financial couch potato's way out, either! Yes, yes...we have credit cards for a reason. But, unless you have a specific, detailed plan for paying off the debts you already have, I wouldn't wager that you're currently in a good space to dive even deeper into the red.

In order to pursue Moratorium, you need to work toward eliminating unnecessary stressors in your life. For me, it is difficult to practice Fine while living paycheck-to-paycheck. However, I know that Ivan and I are living below our means in order to make our long-term dream life a reality. So, I lean into feelings of financial insecurity today so that I can eliminate financial worries in the future. I am working toward "Financial Fine" each day, while simultaneously improving my relationship with the idea of wealth and telling myself often that we can do what we have set our minds to.

And so can *you*!

As a side note, you may have noticed that my Very Specific Dream about James Corden requires both money *and* fame, and that I have only thus far mentioned my need for money. As for the fame part -- well, speaking as the former little girl who literally couldn't bear to *not* be in a single home movie...that one's just for fun. :)

A Book to Read or Listen to... *You Are a Badass: How to Stop Doubting Your Greatness and Start Living an Awesome Life* by Jen Sincero

Chapter #13:

The Oven Ain't Broke

You know that episode of *SpongeBob SquarePants* where SpongeBob has to write an essay for his boating school teacher, Mrs. Puff, and he gets himself so worked up with writer's block that he can't think of anything to write except an intricately calligraphic "The"?

Well, my friends...

The.

The thing is...I am here to tell you that, despite my better judgement and abundant cognitive assurances that I should not be, I find that I *am* significantly nervous to write about this topic. I have been lectured, yelled at, side-eyed, and scorned for what I'm about to proclaim. However, I am actively working to recognize this internalized fear as everyone else's problem...well, I suppose that's an exaggeration. It truly is, though, the problem of the people who have a *problem* with it. It's not my issue at all, so I will henceforth absolve myself from any responsibility or anxiety for it.

Okay. Here goes!

I DON'T WANT TO HAVE KIDS.

Let me qualify this statement, in the short, quiet space I have between the time steam comes out of your great-aunt's ears and a well-meaning mom in the throws of breastfeeding coos a knowing cliche.

I am not necessarily saying that I never want to raise children, ever, period, the end. I can see it now -- in ten years, I've changed my mind and had a child, and everyone who has read this book will shout insults at her in the streets:

Your mother never wanted you!

She said she never wanted kids, not long before you were born. You must have been an "oops"!

We read it in her book, which was a New York Times Bestseller and part of Oprah's Book Club -- of course we took her at her word!

Hold. The. Motorola Razr. Phone.

What I am saying is that I *might* not want to raise children, ever. But I *definitely* don't want to push a human out my middle hole, I can guaran-damn-tee you that. Sure, I might end up serving as a foster mom, or an adoptive parent. And, equally as likely (or more), I might not. My husband and I have talked and talked about this issue. And the truth of it is, having children does not align with our current life goals as a couple -- and we are fiercely committed to these goals.

These visions and dreams have evolved over the years, and they are growing bigger still. But we have the tenacity to do what's necessary in pursuit of what we want, and you will notice rather quickly that nowhere on our to-do list does it read, "Have a baby." So here's our plan, in a nutshell (check back with me in a couple years to see how our progress is coming along):

Dani & Ivan's Life Goals (circa 2019):

1. Move to Flagstaff, AZ

    o We want to live here so badly, it's literally the only thing besides legally required healthcare that's keeping us currently toiling away at full-time jobs. In order to reach this goal, we are smashing our debts, fixing up our house, scouring Realtor.com, and budgeting in multiple trips in the near future to visit our "forever home" before we move there permanently. We both plan to go back to school to earn Master's degrees and will eventually land glamorous jobs that we love, both of which will allow us to see each other disgustingly often. In fact, we'd really prefer to work together every day.

2. Travel the World

    o Using Flagstaff as the world's most gorgeous, nature-filled, and physically active Home Base, Ivan and I will springboard our way to the ends of the earth, seeing as many parts of it (and meeting as many of its people) as humanly possible. We *love* to travel, but thus far we have experienced it only through the eyes of paupers. For example, on our honeymoon, we toured New York City and ate at...McDonald's, even though we *wanted* fancy cheesecake (but for $14? Nah, that's 14 McChickens, so...). In our future, we will fly to extravagant places and dine with local friends, whose perspectives and customs will change our lives irrevocably. This dream, both delectable and financially charged, leads me to Goal #3.

3. Get Rich!

    ○ Have you ever wished you could surprise a bubbly and attentive waitress with a 500% tip? Have you ever pined for the freedom to leave work unexpectedly to visit a friend across the country (or the world) who was just having the worst week ever? Did you ever think, in real, quantitative terms, how much good you could do in the world, in small but consequential steps, if you had more money? (Also...have you ever wished you could just buy the damned full-price shoes without feeling guilty? *How pretentious, right?*) The simple truth is, I WANT MONEY! I want lots of it, and I want the freedom that comes with the disappearance of financial stress. Oh, come now Susan, I know that money won't solve my problems. But it will afford me the freedom to help ease the problems of others, and it will also allow me to be more comfy and buy beautiful, substantial things so as to achieve Goal #2 (see above).

A Tissue for Your Issue

So, what is the problem with having these goals? Nothing, from my perspective, but there is the minor problem of middle-aged men pointing (I'm not joking, literally *pointing*) at my uterus, muttering things like, *You'll change your mind. Having kids is the best thing you could experience in life. Lolz, is this your funny way of announcing that you're already pregnant?*

Sigh.

I know that most of these people (particularly those whom we love and who love us) have the best intentions and perhaps are simply reacting to the feeling that they are losing out on some projected experience of our potential future offspring. They desire to witness a little Hartung cherub grow, and I respect that. But I also think, on the other hand, that it is just about the worst idea of all time to procreate solely for the appeasement of others. Does this not sound like a recipe for resentment, or am I missing something?

Besides simply *not* being bothered by tradition, we have come to terms with the fact that, even if we wanted to "settle down and start pumping out the chitlins" like society would have us do, it could potentially take us about thirteen lifetimes to achieve our other goals. Oh, yes, there are those parents who reside on One Percent Boulevard, who can take their six children to Rome for Spring Break, and make a quick stop at Saks Fifth Avenue on the way home to Los Angeles. But literally none of that scenario sounds appealing to me. If we ever were to even consider adoption as a possibility (maybe *especially* if we chose adoption, considering the expense), we will already be living in the city and home we want to be in for the entire foreseeable future.

I've seen it too many times -- a couple starts out with aspirations and plans and a feasible budget, and then....miracle of miracles, they selflessly put all these things on hold to care for their little bundle of joy. I mean none of this sarcastically, by the way. Babies are miracles! But my mom always says, "Everything in life's a trade-off," and that rings true when deciding whether or not to bear children. Personally, I'm not willing to make that trade. And this doesn't make me "selfish" or "delusional." Unfortunately, it also doesn't make other people mind their damn business.

The Choice is Mine: Finding Your Fine

In essence, just because my body came preloaded with birthing features I was not able to opt out of, doesn't mean I am *obligated* to create life by cooking a human in my gut. Here's the thing -- I respect the living hell out of moms! I think it is a beautiful thing to give birth and commit your life to raising a child and putting yourself second because you love this little creature so much that you would give your life to protect her. I think that it is honorable and praiseworthy and good to choose a life of parenthood.

What I would really appreciate is some motherfuckin' reciprocity! Why can't we respect and revere the lives of couples who choose to live out their days in a different, childless form of service? It's not that I don't love kids -- I *love* them! Being "Aunt Dani" is one of the most heart-filling honors of my existence, and I know that in a previous lifetime, as well as in the future of this one, I was and will be the happiest elementary school teacher there ever was.

On the other hand, I want to set this world on fire with my curiosity, tenacity, and love for instruction and presentation. I want to "pick up and go" wherever this life takes me. And as strongly as I feel this urge to spread my wings, what I don't feel is the steady *tick-tick-tick* of my biological clock, reminding me that it's time to utilize my flesh oven. I just don't. I don't have that longing or feel that calling, and it would be so, so awesome if everyone would just respond with, "That's nice, dear," instead of, "WHAT?! Why not? You guys would make the BEST parents!"

And, yes, I say to the grouchy cynic in the back, I am fully aware that some people who *want* babies are not physiologically able to have them. This tragedy is not lost on me. However, the burden of righting this apparent injustice is also not mine to bear. My gleefully impregnating my womb does not help these mommy and daddy hopefuls to become pregnant any faster, or at all. It does not settle some cosmic score for me to bear forth the fruit of Hartung loins, in the name of gratitude for my fortuitously fertile eggs.

What I am learning from the ongoing experience of being a purposefully barren, married spindler -- and what I would like for you to learn with me -- is that even the most deep-rooted expectations of society are, for the most part, utter bullshit. You don't have to buy in to the narrative that "Women can be as successful as they want to be, but they'd also better give their king a son!" You don't have to, and it's *fine*!

The truth is, maybe your "thing" isn't that you don't want to have kids. Maybe your "thing" is that you want to start your own business, or move to Wyoming and become a full-time white water rafting instructor, or shave your head. You know what? All of these choices are *choices*, and any one of them can help you to live a very Fine life. And if one of these (or something completely different) resonates with you, then that means the Universe is telling you something, friend! Explore that inner wish!

Take a good look at your truth. Figure out what you want to do, who you want to be -- and identify the "why" for each of your goals. I want to move to Flagstaff because it's beautiful and surrounded by national parks and at a high altitude, resulting in a blissfully mild climate. It's also beautiful to have a goal that Ivan and I are working on side-by-side, toward the future we have dreamed up together. Why do you want to do *your* thing? Is that reasoning strong enough to combat the middle-aged men who will inevitably point at your shaved head and exclaim, "But WHY? You had such beautiful curls!"?

Prep yourself for others to mistrust *your* guiding light. But you're not hurting anyone by living your best life, on your own terms. And when they say things like that to you?

Your answer needs to be, "HELL YES IT IS. BRING IT ON, BECAUSE I FEEL FINE".

A Book to Read or Listen to... *How I Live Now* by Meg Rosoff

Chapter #14:
On Pooping and Personal Positives

On our first extended road trip together (after dating for a couple of months), Ivan and I had a brilliant time in St. Louis, Missouri. We paid a visit to the zoo, followed by a stroll in the nearby park -- finding out along the way that both of us loved willow trees! -- and then capped off the afternoon with a self-guided tour of the local art gallery. It was absolutely magical!

On our journey back to the motel, however, Ivan's face grew crimson and grim. "My...my tummy's bubblin' all of a sudden," he said, sounding for the first time like he wished with all his might that I wasn't there with him. I grinned and asked the same question school teachers ask on Knock-Off-McRib Day: "Do you need to use the restroom?"

Now, by this point in our relationship, Ivan and I had most definitely broken the fart barrier; in fact, that didn't take long at all. One threshold we had not crossed, however, was the one we were about to be hilariously and unforgettably forced over. I rushed after my sprinting bae from the car to the room, where a small, paper-thin-walled bathroom awaited him. He turned on the music as loud as his phone would play One Direction...and then ensued the absolute massacre of our poor, unsuspecting toilet.

One-hundred honking geese dropping missile bombs onto a trumpet players' convention during a raging thunderstorm could not have compared to the symphony of sound emerging from that bathroom. "I'm so sorry, Dani!" he shrieked between pushes and grunts, and I laughed harder than I had ever *laughed, up to that point in my life. To this day, this is one of our funniest and most treasured memories.*

....

I have, a time or two in my life, been embarrassingly duped by a first impression. This misjudgement can feasibly (and historically) go in either direction, meaning that sometimes I over-love a person upon first meeting them, and other times I immediately over-hate. In either case, however, I have found only one first-glance metric indicative of genuine, long-lasting trustworthiness and valor in another human being. This test has yet to fail me, and I would like to share it in the hopes that you will utilize its fortune-telling power to better both your life and the greater world. I have discovered that I can only fully rely on a person if...

If I can talk to them about poop.

Now, at first glance, this sounds like a some cheap, dumb bathroom humor (pun intended). But hear me out -- this is actually one of the truest truths you'll read all day, guaranteed.

Despite its bad rep as an immature topic of conversation, pooping is actually one of the most natural, human things that we do every day (or, at least, hopefully on a regular basis). Poop stinks, which is good, because that stench discouraged our ancestors from eating or decorating with it; however, pooping on the reg actually means you're in good health! Isn't that something worth sharing with friends? If I am praised for sharing my favorite lemon chicken lentil soup recipe on social media, why am I considered "gross" for also mentioning the monster butt birth it caused?

In high school, talking about poop in the locker room was a sign of camaraderie and trust. It was understood that we were going to have to drop deuces in pretty close quarters, and so it was deemed forgivable to be stinky, so long as you didn't judge the next person's rank rip. You also got bonus points if you were open enough to warn your teammates of impending nasal barrage of E. Coli. "Don't go into stall number two for at least twenty minutes," I'd proclaim. "I just totally fuckin' destroyed it."

Once in college, I quickly began to exchange secrets with friends about the "best pooping spots" on campus. Nowadays, I like to rank my diet suggestions based on how well they aid me in keepin' it regular. In other words, though my interest in poop has evolved from the juvenile to the health-conscious, I still find it a very reliable metric with which to measure a person's trustworthiness and eventual comfortability with less-than-tasteful business.

To put it lightly, in other words, MY kind of people are POOPIE people.

I think that it is such an egregious and ungrateful waste of time to make others feel bad or embarrassed over their basic human needs. People literally *have* to poo! But this principal extends far beyond the jurisdiction of the porcelain throne. The type of friend who doesn't make nasty comments about your bowel aroma is generally also the type of friend who won't judge you during an anxiety attack. They are likely going to be the friend who is there for you, reassuring and validating you when you're planning a wedding and don't want to "bother anyone" with the details. He will sing Disney songs at the top of his lungs with you after a long and stressful week of work.

These are your POOPIE friends -- in the best way! And that type of friendship encourages the purposeful practice of Fine. Moratorium can be reached in the company of these friends, because they encourage you with grace and without judgement. And they also cook dinners full of hidden chia seeds for you, when they're worried that you might be a little backed up.

I would highly encourage you to seek out and identify the friends in your life who are comfy with the yucky, because nine times out of ten, they will be cool with the emotionally awkward as well. People who don't take themselves (or their friends' butts) too seriously are my favorite, because they innately understand the concept of Fine on a level that I took years and lots of unnecessary embarrassment to achieve. They realize that people are beautiful *because* of their perceived flaws, not just in spite of them. They appreciate those around them for the imperfect examples of love that they are, and they (sometimes unknowingly) guide their friends toward peace and an elevated sense of self-worth simply by confirming that natural, albeit unseemly, bodily functions don't dampen their love in the slightest.

Great buds won't just pat you on the back when you killed it in this week's drinking game (though they still might). They will be there to hold your hair back when you're not sure which end of you is about to projectile. And they'll reassure you that you're pretty and smart and no, not annoying at all! Friends like this help you to identify and hold onto what one of my former supervisors referred to as "Personal Positives."

Your Personal Positives are things you notice, do, say, and know about yourself throughout the course of each day that make you happy or proud.

These things can range from your choice of outfit to the amazingly beautiful weather, but they reflect what makes *you* feel high vibe and upbeat. If a friend consistently finds ways to help you notice and appreciate your Personal Positives, either through pep talks or an optimistic example, then they are a great force to have around you.

Notice stuff like this -- and, through all your friendship analysis, understand that not every friend will be this for you, and that's okay! Friendships are like snowflakes, in that each one is special and unique, and filled with just a tiny bit of dirt. None are "perfect"! Some friendships melt away quickly, while others linger on and continue to shine. Some are fun, but you wouldn't want them around all the time.

The Choice is Mine: Finding Your Fine

This is all my drawn-out, funny way of saying something I have found to be very important to my practice of Fine:

You need friends -- but what you *really* need are *good* friends.

In order to search for Moratorium within yourself and your own life, and in order to practice your very own version of Fine, you will need people in your corner who are accepting, loving, and patient. Don't make friends with someone if your only common interest is making fun of Sharon, from the marketing team. Allow people to see you for who you are -- be vulnerable! But don't be naive, either. You need to see people for who *they* are, and build your tribe of friends based on who is there for you in the moments that count.

Who is interested in meeting your little brothers and playing with your dogs? Who buys the kind of gum you like because she knows that it calms you down and you *always* forget to buy it? Who helps you to complete your daily affirmations, even when you don't feel worthy to practice them? Who helps you to experience your Personal Positives? There are many different types of friendships, so you might have one bestie, or each of those scenarios may have brought to mind a different, awesome pal. The point is, you DESERVE -- Ya hear me? *Deserve.* -- good, wonderful friendships in your life. You deserve to be loved unconditionally by amazing friends who build you up and keep you grounded.

You have to decide for yourself who those friends are, and how to find them. For me, it starts with something as simple as their reaction to an explosive little four-letter word.

A Book to Read or Listen to... *The Strange Case of Origami Yoda* by Tom Angleberger

Chapter #15:
My Very Own Alphabet Rug

I glance purposefully across the room, at the student who is projecting armpit fart noises in order to make his classmates giggle. A raised eyebrow in his direction is all it takes to elicit a sheepish, eyes-to-the-floor grin, accompanied by a mumbled, "Sorry, Mrs. Hartung." I smile mischievously in his direction, and his gaze reaches back up to meet mine. "It's funny, but it doesn't belong in school!" I say, trying my best to sound stern and hide my grin. He chuckles and answers, "I knooooow," and goes back to his art project.

I sigh wistfully as I return to the next student, whose question I still haven't answered amid all the chaos. She is waiting patiently for my attention, but she is also picking her nose, just a tiny bit. We chat about hand sanitizer and correct a spelling error, and then the bell rings for lunch.

This is my classroom. This is my career. I am a teacher.

....

For what seems like eons, my heart has yearned to become a teacher...and, though I haven't achieved this goal as of yet, I am still just as "on fire" for teaching as I have ever been. It has been (is) a long road, but I know that I will make it happen -- and it is this determination, to me, that demonstrates my steadfast commitment to my own dreams. On the other hand, it is my contentedness with the present moment that helps me to find Moratorium in the everyday life on the road to this very dream.

When I graduated high school in 2011, I was honestly terrified of children. They were so *breakable* and unpredictable...and loud! Of course, older kids (junior high and high school students) were no problem. Younger kiddos, though -- ranging in age from newborns to about fifth graders -- were scary to me, because I didn't feel that I knew how to properly act around them. Both of my siblings and most of my cousins were born within a few years of me, and those who were a bit younger, I didn't see as much growing up. I left for college hoping to become a secondary education Social Studies teacher; so, the spark for teaching existed already...but definitely not for the young-uns.

After meeting with my college advisor for the first time, I suddenly decided that I most definitely did *not* want to become a high school Social Studies teacher. The classes looked incredibly dull to me when written out, bulleted list-style, on the paper she kindly slid across her desk in my direction. I promptly set out to select a different major, one that better suited my interests of the time. I looked through every program offered at my institution (except, I remember distinctly, "anything related to agriculture"). What I found, and subsequently chose, would immediately alter the trajectory of my life.

I chose Communication Studies, a major that I enjoyed every waking minute of. My department was small, very small relative to others on campus, so even though I attended a larger state university, I got to know my professors on a first-name basis. As one might assume a group of people dedicated to studying human communication might be, my teachers and advisors were patient, funny, kind, and incredibly intelligent. I worked closely with several of them, most notably my senior mentor, whose guidance and mentorship made me both a more avid student and well-rounded woman of academia. Sadly, the signs became increasingly clearer over the course of my tenure in the department of "Comm" that I was not meant to follow in her footsteps and become a professor and researcher.

One day, while walking on campus in 2012, I vividly remember seeing a small child playing with their parents in the quad area, between academic buildings. I didn't know this child, or really pay much attention to the scene, until the kid stared directly at me, smiled, and waved! I called my mom during my walk (something I did pretty incessantly throughout college) and recounted the story for her, overly excited that a child was not only unafraid of me, but that they had actually *smiled* and acknowledged my existence! Maybe, I thought, things were turning around for me in the kid department. Maybe one day I wouldn't be so scared of them. In the meantime, I had lots of other obligations to distract me.

At one such event, my destiny came calling. Every fall, our track team would host a Sunday meet for local high school students and children who had signed up for traveling club teams in the area. It was always a great turnout, and lots of fun (as long as you didn't get stuck working the check-in table, which was unbearably dull). In 2013, I was assigned to help measure distances for shot put throws. This meant that I had to pull the end of a measuring tape from the back of the throwing circle after every contestants' attempt, trying hard to focus both on accurate measurement and *not* showing off my thong underwear to the crowd each time I crouched down to pull the tape taut.

As we moved along to the younger age divisions, one little girl (who couldn't have been older than five) walked gingerly and nervously over to the ring. She held the tiniest shot put I had ever seen and, judging from the uncomfortable look on her face, she wished that she was literally anywhere else in the world at that moment. She started to whimper and whine something about how she "didn't know what to do," and her older sister (who was also competing) tried with gusto to explain the event to her tiny sibling. Though I was technically working as an event official, my heart went out to the poor girl, and I asked her if she had ever thrown the shot put before. When she shook her head no, I thanked her sister and said that I would take it from there.

I helped the girl by showing her how to hold the implement and *heave*, rather than "throw," it. I reminded her to exit out of the back half of the circle so that her mark could be counted, and I encouraged her after each attempt. By the end of the competition, I'm pretty certain I had *not* convinced the girl to love throwing. But a small spark had ignited in my heart that day -- one that never, ever went out.

Later that year, in the springtime, I was hired to coach for our own local club team. I was in charge of shot put and discus throwers, between the ages of 8 and 18. I absolutely *loved* this job! To this day, it is one of my most treasured experiences. Through this coaching gig, which I really started just to earn a little bit of extra money on the side, I made lifelong friends (and worked the first of several jobs alongside my future husband, who wasn't even my boyfriend yet at the time).

This same school year (2013 was evidently a big year for me), I also began working as a lunchroom attendant at an elementary school in town. Basically, my job was to lose any semblance of good hearing, while patrolling the roaring lunchroom filled with a couple hundred students at a time. I was to help them open milk cartons, line up for tray dumping, and remember to follow the school's rules.

This experience was my first, albeit rudimentary, taste of "classroom management," in that attendants like myself had to use multiple call-and-response techniques in order to convey information to such large groups of students. In addition, we had to learn how to convince mobs of sixth-graders to behave in line while remaining (relatively) quiet and respectful. It was a madhouse, and I had an absolute blast.

One afternoon, while driving home from my lunchroom shift, I called my dad, who has been a teacher and coach for just longer than I've been alive. I told him that I'd changed my mind, and that I knew now what I wanted to do with my life. I wanted to be just like him, I explained. I wanted to be an elementary school teacher and coach, and I heard the emotion in my generally stoic father's voice as he excitedly encouraged me to follow this dream career path, which he believed I would truly love and be successful in. That Christmas, he gave me one of the most special and personal gifts I have ever received -- my first coach's whistle.

Unfortunately, this is the part of the story where my unrequited love for teaching began to take several twists, turns, and pit stops.

When you are a student-athlete in the NCAA, evidently switching majors mid-career is not looked kindly upon. In fact, it can jeopardize your eligibility to compete. When I contacted an advisor about changing my major from Communication Studies to Elementary Education, I was told that, due to percentage-of-completion regulations, this was not a possibility for me, if I wanted to remain on the track team.

In other words, student-athletes must have completed a certain percentage toward their degree for each year of competition. (This is to prevent athletes from taking four years of "fluff" courses to focus on training, and never actually graduating.) If these requirements are not met, the student becomes ineligible for athletic competition. Because of these regulations, switching my major would have put me behind in my total percentage and therefore rendered me unable to continue my track career.

Not wanting to put my shot put dreams in danger, I chose to keep my major the same, vowing that I would pursue Elementary Education after I graduated with my bachelor's degree. Between 2014 and 2016, I continued to work at the elementary school and coach, both for the club team and private, hourly clients. During this time, I earned a 3.9 GPA, passed my Senior Thesis course, and won an NCAA Division-I Indoor National Women's Shot Put Championship.

Throughout all of these experiences, my love for teaching only grew.

After a career-ending injury sent me abruptly off the post-collegiate training path and into the workforce in one fell swoop, I was hired as a special education para, at the very same elementary school I had worked in as a lunchroom aide. From February until May, I worked throughout the school and with several students, namely two boys in the second grade who greatly challenged me...and ensnared my heart forever.

I left this school only because Ivan and I decided to move back to my hometown on the other side of the state. This decision, in turn, was made partly due to the fact that I was denied entry into an Elementary Education master's program (when the admitting professor would not allow me to apply for the cohort while simultaneously working as a graduate assistant for the track team -- the only way that I could have afforded to do it).

Once moved, I worked a brief stint for an organization based in social work and community outreach, but quickly revived my longing to return to the classroom. I gave my two-weeks' notice and enrolled in full-time virtual undergraduate courses, while also taking a job as a full-time preschool para in another small town. I worked this job until the end of the school year, after which I accepted a university admissions counselor position. At this point, I had decided to shelve my teacher-y dreams, because I simply could not financially afford to continue the path that I was on.

In order to be considered for this job, I had to agree to withdraw from my Elementary Education courses, as my required upcoming practicum hours would interfere with my professional travel schedule. I made this agreement because, frankly, admissions counselors make more money than paras do...and I had come to the heartbreaking conclusion that teaching must not be my calling after all. Otherwise, why did every door I knock on seem to slam shut?

Of course, however, after working in my current position for six months or so, I could not shake the sure feeling that I must not give up on my dream of teaching. I scheduled a meeting with the chair of the Teacher Education department, and my whole story spilled out in his office, in some incoherent, babbling string of sentences. After several meetings, he shared with me that our university had been approved for a non-traditional path to licensure, via a brand-new cohort program. I burst into tears of joy in his office -- finally, a door was opening!

I am happy to announce that I plan to pursue this new program, which I will be starting in the upcoming summer term. I do not just dream about becoming a teacher and having my own classroom ("with my very own alphabet rug!" as I often exclaim to my friends). I *know* that I *will* become a teacher, because it is what I was meant to be. In fact, I often have vivid Futuries about the road to Mrs. Hartung's Classroom:

....

I stand at the front of the room, with my dad sitting at a table, in a chair next to me. In front of us stand friends, family, and co-workers who have helped me to get to this point with their encouragement, advice, and patience. I hand an envelope to my dad, who opens it with an emotional smile and signature chuckle. Inside, he finds a printed copy of my official teaching license, and I laugh and hug him, while we both cry tears of joy, over the years and hard work and road blocks we have overcome together, in order to achieve this moment.

The Choice is Mine: Finding Your Fine

In my more intellectually stable moments, I try to consider that life is a series of "This-Because-of-This" moments. Basically, while I still maintain fundamental disagreement with the statement, "Everything happens for a reason," I *do* believe that some things either do or don't happen in order to allow room for other events and experiences to take place. While this forward motion is driven largely by free-will *decisions*, sometimes things that seem impossible or unlikely are only kept from us for a time, so that they might be presented differently later on.

In my case, I have been frustrated, disappointed, and even heartbroken by the winding road that has led me to this point in my pursuit of a teaching career. Even still, though, I cannot say that I would change my unique path, because it has led me to some very formative experiences and allowed for amazing friendships and networking opportunities to grow.

I still believe, exactly as I did on the day I called my dad from the car to tell him that I wanted to be just like him, that teaching is my true calling and contribution to the world. However, I know that this will happen in the proper time, and I have to work to find Moratorium in the interim moments until it occurs.

I have to remind myself that "*This* happened because *This* happened before it," in order to keep my perspective positive and not lose heart. This mindset, however, is a constant work in progress, as it can be increasingly difficult to release my grip on the timeline of the Universe and remember that, no matter where I end up, I will be absolutely *Fine*.

Think about it for a minute. In what ways can you "let go" of the way you thought your dreams would look? I know that this may sound counter-intuitive, after all the Vision Board talk and dream-big advice I've offered thus far. But it's crucial to remember that, sometimes, we don't get exactly what we want, when or *how* we desire it. Sometimes, there is intrinsic value in the Very Specific Dreams that supersedes their actualization. You *need* to dream, you *need* to plan, and you *need* to believe in yourself. But your Fine is not damaged or revoked when goals and visions *change* and *evolve*. You owe it to yourself to hold tight to your dreams, while rooting yourself wholly to the beauty of the journey, regardless of where it appears you are headed.

A Book to Read or Listen to... *Roadmap to Responsibility* by Larry Thompson

Chapter #16:

How I Purposefully Practice "Fine"

PSA: I am fully convinced that social media organizations are run by psychics -- or, if this is even possible, by money-hungry empaths.

Either that, or they are run by the world's best guessers and most sympathetic and manipulative listeners. The reason I believe this is because every time I "like," share, or watch something…my news or search engine feed is suddenly full of other, similar items. From what I understand, this generating and re-ordering of my automated content is courtesy of what's known as an *algorithm*, or statistically driven formula implemented to make my online experience more personally (and profitably) enticing.

The funny thing is, my "frequently-visited content" isn't always made up of things I actually *like*. Sometimes, I spend my time online watching frustrating political videos that make me lose faith in humanity. Other times, I scroll through the comments of a controversial post, just to witness the proverbial "fireworks show" of mudslinging, tomfoolery and general disrespect. Or, when I'm feeling particularly saucy, I will watch (on mute, you best believe) a whole, entire horror movie trailer. In other words, sometimes what I pour into the algorithm is pure, harmful, and self-inflicted *filth*.

But the algorithm doesn't know that! It can't differentiate between what I enjoy watching and what I consume on days when I'm simply a glutton for punishment. Because of this, I have to be on guard for my own well-being. There are days when I have to actually go through my social media accounts and purify them, as best I can, of the grime that the algorithm has perpetuated. I have to rifle through my newsfeed and make sure my "likes" and "follows" are in line with what I am prepared and excited to see as I scroll through my account each day.

I have to practice self-care by refusing to follow or be electronic friends with certain people I actually *know* in real life, because I know myself well enough to recognize my tendency to take on and internalize the emotions of others. If someone is spewing hate-drenched drivel all over my daily perusal of the Web, then I have to realize the harm this does to me -- and *then* I have to make myself a priority by removing them from my immediate lines of vision and thought.

In other words, I have to pluck their energy from my algorithm.

I have to consciously gather the courage to stand up for myself (courage which is not always readily available, as anyone who has ever e-replied to their great-uncle's best friend's misogynistic cousin's comment will tell you). Even so, I know that I have to prioritize my own peace of mind by taking out the formulaic trash every now and again. Now, some might argue that I could avoid all this headache and anguish by simply leaving social media altogether. Yes, in theory, I *could* deactivate all of my accounts and permanently disable both my computer and phone -- but how realistic is that? And why cut myself off like that, if it's not necessary or helpful?

No, in my opinion, the key to keeping a healthy perspective on being "plugged in" is an honest practice of prioritization -- and this takes great awareness and practice. In your day-to-day life, the natural energy of the world appears to have an algorithm of its own, which is at least partially dependent on your pattern of choices. The energy you release out into the Universe will trigger it to assume that's what it should add next to your queue. Think of your life like a station on a music streaming device... You can "thumbs-up" and "thumbs-down" songs depending on how much time you want to spend listening to them (regardless of whether you find them truthful and valuable or not; I mean, hey...sometimes bad songs are *catchy*).

So, the Universe will flood your life's station with similar tunes unless you actively change your settings and preferences. You have to remember to scrub your playlist clean when it becomes toxic! Yeah, sure...some days, you need a little scream-o. But do you need that influence in your ears 24/7?

How might one go about this algorithmic improvement? See the list below for ways that I up the positive anty, in everyday ways:

1. Working Out

   - Whether it is lifting weights or playing a game like four square, physical activity has always been a great stress reliever for me. I gleefully collect the endorphins and get high on the accomplishment of a win or new personal best. I also love sports, because they can be taken as seriously as you want; so, I might play a highly competitive softball game, *or* I may opt for a beach-volleyball-and-Smirnoff afternoon with friends.

2. Yoga

   - My view of yoga, over the past several years, has shifted from a mere workout to a deeply profound method of connecting to myself and creating a habit of love, confidence, and Moratorium. I find that, when I do yoga every day (even if it's only for five minutes), I am happier, calmer, and more self-assured.

3. Meditation

- This one was a little bit difficult for me to get into. After reading the book *10% Happier* by Dan Harris, I felt compelled to begin a meditation practice of my own. Although I have yet to get nearly as in-depth and committed as the author, I noticed that mind-clearing meditation (focusing solely on the in-and-out motion of the breath) has helped me to practice being centered and in tune with my body's functionality, which has helped me to stay grounded in stressful situations.

4. Singing and Songwriting

- I looooove to sing! I have enjoyed singing for as long as I can remember. And for just about that long, I have been trying my hand at writing poetry and song lyrics. While I wouldn't mind at all if one of my YouTube videos caught fire and went viral, right now it's a fine hobby that brings me joy and allows me the satisfaction of arranging syllables and rhymes to my content.

5. Writing

- Writing is one of my greatest loves in this life. When I was younger, my parents encouraged me to use writing to work through my emotions and feelings, especially when I was having a difficult time verbalizing them. Eloquence became my emotional currency, and I fell head-over-thesaurus in love with the process of creative writing. Ever since the fifth grade, I have dreamed of turning this pastime into authorship!

6. Deep, Energetic Talks Over Coffee Shared (DETOCS)

    - I have created this play on the word "detox" to illustrate just how powerful and restorative a coffee convo can be. Realistically, "coffee" can be interchanged with "wine," "water," or "chocolate milk," but the point is that genuine, focused conversations with friends (especially one-on-one) tend to bring me great clarity, reassurance, and feelings of camaraderie and safety.

The Choice is Mine: Finding Your Fine

I visited a high school last semester who was celebrating one of the most interesting "holidays" I'd ever heard of. They called it "Grati-Tuesday," as it was the last day of classes before the Thanksgiving break. I found this idea both cute and philosophically weighty, and I decided to make it a regular practice for myself.

In the coming year, I am going to commit to a small, personal Grati-Tuesday celebration each and every week. This doesn't have to be anything fancy; rather, it just means that I will take the time each Tuesday to identify something that I am thankful for and meditate on it for a few minutes. Then, I will share it with my friends, maybe even using the social media hashtag #GratiTuesday.

In this way, I am making a tiny, yet significant step in my own gratitude practice. I will improve my spiritual algorithm by amping up the positive content I consume, and I will purposefully practice Fine through my concentrated thankfulness meditation.

Would you like to join me? Although punny hashtags make me feel happy, I also ascribe to the yoga teacher Adriene Mishler's mantra: Find What Feels Good. Adriene is quick to remind viewers of her Yoga With Adriene channel that "FWFG" is "not a free-for-all" but rather a deeply personal search for the yoga pose variation (read: lifestyle choice) that best suits each individual person.

So, I invite you to join me on my GratiTuesday quest, or find what other type of algorithm improvement feels good to *you*. Maybe you want to keep a gratitude journal, or send a thank-you card, or say a prayer. You might be surprised at what new suggestions the Universe comes up with for your life, based on your commitment to these practices of self-care and -love.

A Book to Read or Listen to... *10% Happier* by Dan Harris

Chapter #17:
Conclusion: My Little Teal Chameleon

My collegiate throws coach and I really didn't get along in the beginning (meaning, we actually hated the fact that the other existed). He entered the scene my sophomore year, after my original coach, who was like a second dad to me, changed career paths and left the university altogether. I was hurt and sad and anxious about what this would mean for me...and then, entered Greg.

For some reason that, even today, I can't quite pinpoint, I immediately decided that Greg was no friend to me. Granted, he was a young coach and pretty arrogant when he accepted the position, but something in me dug in its heels and refused to buy into his program or his trust. Needless to say, he didn't take too kindly to this. Thus began a year-long douche-fest pissing contest between teacher and pupil. I found out much later that, at this point, he had legitimately looked into the process for cutting my ass from the team.

Of course, this type of drama was no way to make athletic progress, and I knew it. Slowly (soooo slowly), the fog began to lift, and Greg and I co-formulated this sort of dysfunctional, hilarious banter. For him, I think, this concession was a means of retaining his sanity. For me, it began as a teensy compromise so that I could get on with my career, already. By the time I was a junior, though, we worked together (mostly) like a well-oiled machine. There was no mean insult either of us could use that we hadn't already...meaning that I could shout swear words in aggravation on the way to retrieve my shot put, and then listen attentively to his expert advice upon my return to the ring. We had forged a friendship through the most stubborn of fires, and, though it was definitely not the last time we would butt heads, this unspoken agreement of acceptance made moving through the next several years of competition both more effective and fun.

One of the best and most grounding pieces of advice I gleaned from my time with Greg came from (you guessed it) an argument, in which I was frustrated that my progress wasn't improving at the rate I wanted, despite my best efforts.

"That's the problem!" he retorted, uncapping a dry-erase marker and motioning toward a white board. "Everybody thinks that progress is linear, but it's not. It's really like this--"

He proceeded to draw a large, squiggly mass across the board, with the line going up, down, sideways, backward, curly-cue...and then, in the very last inch of his illustration, he added a small, straight line, projecting at a 45-degree angle from the rest of the messy mass.

"It's like this," he said, "I call it 'The Clusterfuck to the Top'."

Although this sentiment didn't blow my mind at the time (after all, I was pissed!), it has stuck with me over the past six or seven years. I believe that this mantra, The Clusterfuck to the Top, can be applied to many areas of life. What he was saying, in essence, was that you cannot waste time and emotional energy beating yourself up because today's practice wasn't quite as good as yesterday's. That's thinking too small. Zoom out a ways and allow yourself to see that, although you made a micro-regression today, your progress *overall* is headed in the general direction of improvement, which will help you when it counts.

"Look at the big picture," Greg would remind me, over and over again, "and trust the process of your training."

Trust.

That's what *you* have to do, what we all have to do, on the road to Fine and the practice of seeking Moratorium. You have to take a deep breath amidst the cluster, collect your confidence, and be your own guiding voice of reason. For example, if your resolution is to eat healthier (and you do so successfully for six months), it may be tempting to mentally punish yourself for eating poorly over an extended holiday weekend. I mean really, that was *several days* of brownies and white wine, girlfriend!

But if you focus negative energy exclusively on your weekend binge, you will miss the entire point: you have created a healthy lifestyle over the last six-months that has made you an overall healthier *person*. It is these habits you've created that will help motivate you to hit the gym on Monday, and your imperfect "hiccup" is merely one, single downward curl of the dry erase marker. It's not time for victory yet, my dear -- it's time for *trust*!

Trust in your Self and in the affirmations you give yourself each day. Even in those moments when it's hard to believe them, you need to speak that truth into the mirror or whisper it quietly to your heart.

If you decide that you're going to walk your dog three times a week, every week, then you have set an awesome goal! If at first, you are only able to carve out the time to walk him once or twice, then you are a human being. Life got in the way? Strategize your schedule better next week! You felt tired and run-down? Get some extra rest this weekend. You have made a commitment to your doggo, but you have to fill *your* cup in order to get there -- and you have to view the fulfillment of that promise as a *process*. Don't give up; TRUST!

And in the interim, while you're creating a habit of self-trust and struggling against the impending tide that is both doubt and insecurity, search for Moratorium. As a reminder, this simply means finding little moments, small pockets of your day, in order to recharge your love batteries and blanket yourself in peace. For me, this looks like yoga and meditation. For you, it may look like listening to jazz music, drinking chamomile tea, or interpretive dancing. These activities are mindful, they are multi-sensory, and they are filled with a joy and steadiness necessary for and specific to *you*.

On the day that I became the NCAA Division-I Indoor National Women's Shot Put Champion, I could have cared less about all the times I'd cried in my car after practice. Any memories of injury and rehab faded into the background. I giggled and posed for pictures and emitted a great sigh of relief. I hadn't done it on my own; I had an amazing support system that helped me to remember who I was and why I was pursuing this dream. With their help, I had learned to trust. I had made it through the clusterfuck and emerged on the other side. And I had done it for *me*.

The Choice is Mine: Finding Your Fine

It doesn't have to be New Year's Eve for you to commit to a new resolution. Take a moment to connect to the deepest desires of your soul -- no really, do it. Meditate for a few moments on the thought of your most intimate desires. What are they, and what are your motivations for them? Will they make you truly happy? Then, surround yourself with a mob of supportive family, friends, and mentors who will genuinely push you toward these goals, while keeping you grounded and "zoomed out" to focus on macro-level progress.

The purposeful practice of Fine is not about the immediate cut-off of all self-doubt or the elimination of any and all steps backward. It is merely a peace with your present situation, and a presence within that peace. Lean into your feelings and acknowledge them. Then, remind yourself that these feelings do not necessarily constitute *truth* and that you are doing *fine*. Do activities that allow you to reach your own, specific state of Moratorium throughout each day, and strive hard to speak your affirmations on a regular basis.

Be a chameleon, but not the kind that blends into its background for the sake of others' comfort. Be a *teal* chameleon! Or a pink, sparkly one -- or emerald, or purple, or orange. Be the type of chameleon who flaunts that weirdly awesome curly tail, looks at the haters on either side of you (*simultaneously*, bitch!), and says, "This is who I am. I am beautiful!" Stand out, because you are one-of-a-kind, and you have something to boast that will be your own, unique ticket to happiness. Now your job is to figure out *what* that "something" is, and to wield it like a magic wand, improving the lives of others by sprinkling them all over with your fairy dust of awesome.

Love yourself! After all, this is the only way that this endeavor will be sustainable, because a labor of love always seems "worth it." And remember that this work will not move in a linear motion; treat yourself with grace during the cluster and, more often than you want to, give your burdens to your Tomorrow Self to deal with. It may take your whole life to reach the consistent level of Moratorium that you aim for, and that is more than okay. In fact, throughout this process of loving yourself and continuously growing, try to joyfully *go with* whatever you feel you need, over however much time that takes.

Please know, from the bottom of my heart and across the Universe to yours:

It is absolutely, positively FINE.

A Book to Read or Listen to... *Miss Peregrine's Home for Peculiar Children* by Ransom Riggs

Epilogue:
These Are My Minutes

Throughout the writing and editing of this book, I have been shocked and pleasantly surprised at the resilience of the human spirit (in particular, my own). At times, I read through its chapters and wonder, "How did I get from *there* to *here*?" I have been challenged and frustrated by the rate of my own progress one day, and then amazed and impressed at reaching my own milestones the next. The difference, I suppose, lies in perspective -- and, most importantly, the act of allowing our human selves to grow and change.

The truth is, you cannot hope to change your life for the better while constantly focusing on the worst aspects of it. Of *course*, you have to feel your feelings and never suppress genuine discontent. To ignore these emotions will only cause them to fester in a deeper and darker place. But, as Dan Harris learned on his own journey of meditation and mindfulness...if these feelings don't *serve* you, then they aren't worth the time and emotional energy it takes to continuously cultivate them. Therefore, they certainly won't lead you to Moratorium!

I have spent the time in which I wrote this book seeking Moratorium in my own life. Remember, this concept is simply the idea that we can reach a place of calm, security, and love *within* ourselves, independent of the approval or validation of others, and even on the days when it's difficult to practice self-care. It is the notion that we can feel (and purposefully practice) Fine as a construct of our own design. Fine is, essentially, a decision. It is a choice made, each day, to try again...to love every single aspect of our entire selves...and to put that love above any other endeavor, because it is the very thing that makes all other ventures both possible and worthwhile. But how do we focus on Fine and seek sustainable Moratorium in a world that is so merciless, noisy, and demanding? We have to forgive ourselves when we falter, and practice self-love unconditionally, and unceasingly.

I was chatting virtually with a dear friend yesterday, in a lovely, hilarious, and heartfelt conversation that was long overdue. Somewhere in the course of our visit, she mentioned another friend of hers who is a mother of two little boys. Some days, this friend feels frustrated, stifled, and "stuck" in her own life. Sometimes, she admittedly experiences moments in which she'd like to change it -- to trade lives for some other, alternate reality in which she doesn't have kids to take care of, or all the responsibilities she currently shoulders. But then, a tiny thought creeps into her mind, and she repeats her favorite mantra:

"These are my minutes."

You see, this courageous woman realizes that, above all, we only get *one* shot at this precious life. We only get one chance, one story, and one heart with which to live it out. We can spend this finite amount of time wishing away our gifts on the days they seem like burdens...but this is futile, both because it is impossible and because it is a depressing method of repaying the Universe for the opportunities we have been given.

Or (and this is a big, massively consequential *or*), we can *dig in*. We can live each day in the hope and pursuit of action which makes us truly and genuinely happy. Maybe it won't tickle us pink *today*, though -- perhaps we have to take a good, long look at what Rachel Hollis calls the difference between "what you want now and what you want *most*." Today might be uncomfortable and anxious and maddening, so that tomorrow or next week or ten years down the road, we can reach our long-term dreams at the end of the cluster journey.

But in those moments -- in the *present* moment -- we have to practice happiness like our life depends on it. Because I am of the firm belief, friends, that it does. On the days you feel ugly because a magazine cover told you so, you only hurt your soul by admonishing it. Your words, your self-treatment, and your attitude can affect the health of your physical body, and even more so your beautiful heart. Why waste the minutes you have by beating up the one person who will *never* leave you? Darling, it's YOU!

In the time since I have finished this manuscript, I have visited Flagstaff, Arizona, for the first time with my husband. We positively loved it and had already begun planning a return trip on the drive home. We made new friends in the area who we plan to stay with the next time we go -- and we visited with a stranger on a walking trail who gave us some great insiders' information on real estate and cost-of-living logistics. We are more on fire than ever to make this dream a reality!

One dream we *have* realized, however, is that of becoming teachers in the same district. This spring, Ivan and I were both offered (and accepted) positions to teach while simultaneously pursuing licensure and master's degrees in our respective areas. He will be teaching K-12 Physical Education, while I will be teaching fifth grade. We could not be more excited! Summer classes have taught us that this two-year road will not be easy...but the passion in our hearts (and a long-term plan) have shown us, conversely, that this is exactly where we are meant to be. We are incredibly thrilled to start this journey, and I have plans brewing for a second book, all about my experience as a first-year teacher!

Additionally, Ivan has given me the gift of a used passport, almost! The other evening, when I came home from one job and had only a few minutes before I had to leave for another, he sent me on an adorable, hand-written scavenger hunt throughout our house. In a large World Atlas that we keep in our living room, I eventually found an envelope, with the words "Please don't be mad..." scrawled across the front. Nervously, I opened it and found money and a page number inside. Turning to the atlas page as instructed, I gasped as I gazed at the geography of Ireland...and, upon looking up at Ivan hopefully, was greeted with the glowing screen of his phone, which lit up with a receipt for international flight tickets, scheduled for next summer. I am still in disbelief, but we are going overseas!

World travel has been a huge goal of ours, ever since we got together six-and-a-half years ago. Our perspective has always been, "Why would we wait until we retire to travel, when there is no guarantee that our bodies and schedules will be able to withstand the strain?" However, I have not been willing to max out credit cards and go on elaborate trips that we can't actually afford. So, Ivan devised a plan. At his current job, he occasionally receives tip money from customers, which he is allowed to keep. For over a year, he secretly hid away most of this cash, sliding it into this envelope to surprise me with *paid-for* tickets.

Romance aside (though this gesture was *insanely* sweet and loving), what impresses me most about Ivan's plan is his steadfast determination and self-discipline. Not only did he have to keep this surprise a secret from me, but he had to keep himself from spending the money on other things, even in the months when finances were tight. He kept his eyes on the prize, born of big-picture love for himself and for me, and this is exactly where Fine is found! This may be a rather extravagant example, but Ivan's dedication to his (and our) dreams is a huge part of the reason they came true. No one plopped free plane tickets on his lap; instead, he worked hard within the means that he had in order to create something meaningful for us both.

Are we going to spend two months at a five-star hotel with a private jet? No, siree Bob! But those aren't things that make us feel Fine. Taking nothing but a backpack and making new friends over a pint in Dublin? Now *that's* more like it! We defined a goal that made us genuinely happy, while fleshing out all the reasons why. And then, we dug in. We waited patiently, while practicing self-love in the meantime, until it was our turn to realize what we'd been planning all along.

We are well aware that two teachers' salaries are not going to buy us a multi-million dollar home and a Hummer collection. But none of that sounds like my idea of an ideal life. What makes me happy is time spent with my love and my pets, new experiences and old friends, financial security, and lots and lots of hiking. I know in my heart why these things make me feel Fine, and all my collective past experiences have taught me that I can make it through to the other side of any goal. But I also know that, even if I don't reach every one of them, it is their mere pursuit which puts me in a prime position to stumble across Moratorium in my everyday life.

This is the experience I choose. This is how I have decided to treat myself: constantly finding my very own version of Fine, while filling my cup with genuine affection so that I can fully love those around me. Working toward what I want, while not getting too attached to the specifics. Seeking Moratorium in my yoga practice, in my grad school courses, and in the cup of coffee I hope to enjoy early tomorrow morning. This is who I want to be, because these are *my* minutes.

How will you spend yours?

Made in the USA
Monee, IL
08 January 2021

56935104R00085